Mometrix
TEST PREPARATION

I0883734

# Series 86/87
## Exam Secrets Study Guide

# Dear Future Exam Success Story

First of all, **THANK YOU** for purchasing Mometrix study materials!

Second, congratulations! You are one of the few determined test-takers who are committed to doing whatever it takes to excel on your exam. **You have come to the right place.** We developed these study materials with one goal in mind: to deliver you the information you need in a format that's concise and easy to use.

In addition to optimizing your guide for the content of the test, we've outlined our recommended steps for breaking down the preparation process into small, attainable goals so you can make sure you stay on track.

We've also analyzed the entire test-taking process, identifying the most common pitfalls and showing how you can overcome them and be ready for any curveball the test throws you.

Standardized testing is one of the biggest obstacles on your road to success, which only increases the importance of doing well in the high-pressure, high-stakes environment of test day. Your results on this test could have a significant impact on your future, and this guide provides the information and practical advice to help you achieve your full potential on test day.

**Your success is our success**

**We would love to hear from you!** If you would like to share the story of your exam success or if you have any questions or comments in regard to our products, please contact us at **800-673-8175** or **support@mometrix.com**.

Thanks again for your business and we wish you continued success!

Sincerely,
The Mometrix Test Preparation Team

**Need more help? Check out our flashcards at:**
**http://MometrixFlashcards.com/Series8687**


Written and edited by the Mometrix Exam Secrets Test Prep Team
Printed in the United States of America

# TABLE OF CONTENTS

# Introduction

**Thank you for purchasing this resource**! You have made the choice to prepare yourself for a test that could have a huge impact on your future, and this guide is designed to help you be fully ready for test day. Obviously, it's important to have a solid understanding of the test material, but you also need to be prepared for the unique environment and stressors of the test, so that you can perform to the best of your abilities.

For this purpose, the first section that appears in this guide is the **Secret Keys**. We've devoted countless hours to meticulously researching what works and what doesn't, and we've boiled down our findings to the five most impactful steps you can take to improve your performance on the test. We start at the beginning with study planning and move through the preparation process, all the way to the testing strategies that will help you get the most out of what you know when you're finally sitting in front of the test.

We recommend that you start preparing for your test as far in advance as possible. However, if you've bought this guide as a last-minute study resource and only have a few days before your test, we recommend that you skip over the first two Secret Keys since they address a long-term study plan.

If you struggle with **test anxiety**, we strongly encourage you to check out our recommendations for how you can overcome it. Test anxiety is a formidable foe, but it can be beaten, and we want to make sure you have the tools you need to defeat it.

# Secret Key #1 – Plan Big, Study Small

There's a lot riding on your performance. If you want to ace this test, you're going to need to keep your skills sharp and the material fresh in your mind. You need a plan that lets you review everything you need to know while still fitting in your schedule. We'll break this strategy down into three categories.

## Information Organization

Start with the information you already have: the official test outline. From this, you can make a complete list of all the concepts you need to cover before the test. Organize these concepts into groups that can be studied together, and create a list of any related vocabulary you need to learn so you can brush up on any difficult terms. You'll want to keep this vocabulary list handy once you actually start studying since you may need to add to it along the way.

## Time Management

Once you have your set of study concepts, decide how to spread them out over the time you have left before the test. Break your study plan into small, clear goals so you have a manageable task for each day and know exactly what you're doing. Then just focus on one small step at a time. When you manage your time this way, you don't need to spend hours at a time studying. Studying a small block of content for a short period each day helps you retain information better and avoid stressing over how much you have left to do. You can relax knowing that you have a plan to cover everything in time. In order for this strategy to be effective though, you have to start studying early and stick to your schedule. Avoid the exhaustion and futility that comes from last-minute cramming!

## Study Environment

The environment you study in has a big impact on your learning. Studying in a coffee shop, while probably more enjoyable, is not likely to be as fruitful as studying in a quiet room. It's important to keep distractions to a minimum. You're only planning to study for a short block of time, so make the most of it. Don't pause to check your phone or get up to find a snack. It's also important to **avoid multitasking**. Research has consistently shown that multitasking will make your studying dramatically less effective. Your study area should also be comfortable and well-lit so you don't have the distraction of straining your eyes or sitting on an uncomfortable chair.

The time of day you study is also important. You want to be rested and alert. Don't wait until just before bedtime. Study when you'll be most likely to comprehend and remember. Even better, if you know what time of day your test will be, set that time aside for study. That way your brain will be used to working on that subject at that specific time and you'll have a better chance of recalling information.

Finally, it can be helpful to team up with others who are studying for the same test. Your actual studying should be done in as isolated an environment as possible, but the work of organizing the information and setting up the study plan can be divided up. In between study sessions, you can discuss with your teammates the concepts that you're all studying and quiz each other on the details. Just be sure that your teammates are as serious about the test as you are. If you find that your study time is being replaced with social time, you might need to find a new team.

# Secret Key #2 – Make Your Studying Count

You're devoting a lot of time and effort to preparing for this test, so you want to be absolutely certain it will pay off. This means doing more than just reading the content and hoping you can remember it on test day. It's important to make every minute of study count. There are two main areas you can focus on to make your studying count.

## Retention

It doesn't matter how much time you study if you can't remember the material. You need to make sure you are retaining the concepts. To check your retention of the information you're learning, try recalling it at later times with minimal prompting. Try carrying around flashcards and glance at one or two from time to time or ask a friend who's also studying for the test to quiz you.

To enhance your retention, look for ways to put the information into practice so that you can apply it rather than simply recalling it. If you're using the information in practical ways, it will be much easier to remember. Similarly, it helps to solidify a concept in your mind if you're not only reading it to yourself but also explaining it to someone else. Ask a friend to let you teach them about a concept you're a little shaky on (or speak aloud to an imaginary audience if necessary). As you try to summarize, define, give examples, and answer your friend's questions, you'll understand the concepts better and they will stay with you longer. Finally, step back for a big picture view and ask yourself how each piece of information fits with the whole subject. When you link the different concepts together and see them working together as a whole, it's easier to remember the individual components.

Finally, practice showing your work on any multi-step problems, even if you're just studying. Writing out each step you take to solve a problem will help solidify the process in your mind, and you'll be more likely to remember it during the test.

## Modality

*Modality* simply refers to the means or method by which you study. Choosing a study modality that fits your own individual learning style is crucial. No two people learn best in exactly the same way, so it's important to know your strengths and use them to your advantage.

For example, if you learn best by visualization, focus on visualizing a concept in your mind and draw an image or a diagram. Try color-coding your notes, illustrating them, or creating symbols that will trigger your mind to recall a learned concept. If you learn best by hearing or discussing information, find a study partner who learns the same way or read aloud to yourself. Think about how to put the information in your own words. Imagine that you are giving a lecture on the topic and record yourself so you can listen to it later.

For any learning style, flashcards can be helpful. Organize the information so you can take advantage of spare moments to review. Underline key words or phrases. Use different colors for different categories. Mnemonic devices (such as creating a short list in which every item starts with the same letter) can also help with retention. Find what works best for you and use it to store the information in your mind most effectively and easily.

# Secret Key #3 – Practice the Right Way

Your success on test day depends not only on how many hours you put into preparing, but also on whether you prepared the right way. It's good to check along the way to see if your studying is paying off. One of the most effective ways to do this is by taking practice tests to evaluate your progress. Practice tests are useful because they show exactly where you need to improve. Every time you take a practice test, pay special attention to these three groups of questions:

- The questions you got wrong
- The questions you had to guess on, even if you guessed right
- The questions you found difficult or slow to work through

This will show you exactly what your weak areas are, and where you need to devote more study time. Ask yourself why each of these questions gave you trouble. Was it because you didn't understand the material? Was it because you didn't remember the vocabulary? Do you need more repetitions on this type of question to build speed and confidence? Dig into those questions and figure out how you can strengthen your weak areas as you go back to review the material.

Additionally, many practice tests have a section explaining the answer choices. It can be tempting to read the explanation and think that you now have a good understanding of the concept. However, an explanation likely only covers part of the question's broader context. Even if the explanation makes perfect sense, **go back and investigate** every concept related to the question until you're positive you have a thorough understanding.

As you go along, keep in mind that the practice test is just that: practice. Memorizing these questions and answers will not be very helpful on the actual test because it is unlikely to have any of the same exact questions. If you only know the right answers to the sample questions, you won't be prepared for the real thing. **Study the concepts** until you understand them fully, and then you'll be able to answer any question that shows up on the test.

It's important to wait on the practice tests until you're ready. If you take a test on your first day of study, you may be overwhelmed by the amount of material covered and how much you need to learn. Work up to it gradually.

On test day, you'll need to be prepared for answering questions, managing your time, and using the test-taking strategies you've learned. It's a lot to balance, like a mental marathon that will have a big impact on your future. Like training for a marathon, you'll need to start slowly and work your way up. When test day arrives, you'll be ready.

Start with the strategies you've read in the first two Secret Keys—plan your course and study in the way that works best for you. If you have time, consider using multiple study resources to get different approaches to the same concepts. It can be helpful to see difficult concepts from more than one angle. Then find a good source for practice tests. Many times, the test website will suggest potential study resources or provide sample tests.

## Practice Test Strategy

If you're able to find at least three practice tests, we recommend this strategy:

### Untimed and Open-Book Practice

Take the first test with no time constraints and with your notes and study guide handy. Take your time and focus on applying the strategies you've learned.

### Timed and Open-Book Practice

Take the second practice test open-book as well, but set a timer and practice pacing yourself to finish in time.

### Timed and Closed-Book Practice

Take any other practice tests as if it were test day. Set a timer and put away your study materials. Sit at a table or desk in a quiet room, imagine yourself at the testing center, and answer questions as quickly and accurately as possible.

Keep repeating timed and closed-book tests on a regular basis until you run out of practice tests or it's time for the actual test. Your mind will be ready for the schedule and stress of test day, and you'll be able to focus on recalling the material you've learned.

# Secret Key #4 – Pace Yourself

Once you're fully prepared for the material on the test, your biggest challenge on test day will be managing your time. Just knowing that the clock is ticking can make you panic even if you have plenty of time left. Work on pacing yourself so you can build confidence against the time constraints of the exam. Pacing is a difficult skill to master, especially in a high-pressure environment, so **practice is vital**.

Set time expectations for your pace based on how much time is available. For example, if a section has 60 questions and the time limit is 30 minutes, you know you have to average 30 seconds or less per question in order to answer them all. Although 30 seconds is the hard limit, set 25 seconds per question as your goal, so you reserve extra time to spend on harder questions. When you budget extra time for the harder questions, you no longer have any reason to stress when those questions take longer to answer.

Don't let this time expectation distract you from working through the test at a calm, steady pace, but keep it in mind so you don't spend too much time on any one question. Recognize that taking extra time on one question you don't understand may keep you from answering two that you do understand later in the test. If your time limit for a question is up and you're still not sure of the answer, mark it and move on, and come back to it later if the time and the test format allow. If the testing format doesn't allow you to return to earlier questions, just make an educated guess; then put it out of your mind and move on.

On the easier questions, be careful not to rush. It may seem wise to hurry through them so you have more time for the challenging ones, but it's not worth missing one if you know the concept and just didn't take the time to read the question fully. Work efficiently but make sure you understand the question and have looked at all of the answer choices, since more than one may seem right at first.

Even if you're paying attention to the time, you may find yourself a little behind at some point. You should speed up to get back on track, but do so wisely. Don't panic; just take a few seconds less on each question until you're caught up. Don't guess without thinking, but do look through the answer choices and eliminate any you know are wrong. If you can get down to two choices, it is often worthwhile to guess from those. Once you've chosen an answer, move on and don't dwell on any that you skipped or had to hurry through. If a question was taking too long, chances are it was one of the harder ones, so you weren't as likely to get it right anyway.

On the other hand, if you find yourself getting ahead of schedule, it may be beneficial to slow down a little. The more quickly you work, the more likely you are to make a careless mistake that will affect your score. You've budgeted time for each question, so don't be afraid to spend that time. Practice an efficient but careful pace to get the most out of the time you have.

# Secret Key #5 – Have a Plan for Guessing

When you're taking the test, you may find yourself stuck on a question. Some of the answer choices seem better than others, but you don't see the one answer choice that is obviously correct. What do you do?

The scenario described above is very common, yet most test takers have not effectively prepared for it. Developing and practicing a plan for guessing may be one of the single most effective uses of your time as you get ready for the exam.

In developing your plan for guessing, there are three questions to address:

- When should you start the guessing process?
- How should you narrow down the choices?
- Which answer should you choose?

## When to Start the Guessing Process

Unless your plan for guessing is to select C every time (which, despite its merits, is not what we recommend), you need to leave yourself enough time to apply your answer elimination strategies. Since you have a limited amount of time for each question, that means that if you're going to give yourself the best shot at guessing correctly, you have to decide quickly whether or not you will guess.

Of course, the best-case scenario is that you don't have to guess at all, so first, see if you can answer the question based on your knowledge of the subject and basic reasoning skills. Focus on the key words in the question and try to jog your memory of related topics. Give yourself a chance to bring the knowledge to mind, but once you realize that you don't have (or you can't access) the knowledge you need to answer the question, it's time to start the guessing process.

It's almost always better to start the guessing process too early than too late. It only takes a few seconds to remember something and answer the question from knowledge. Carefully eliminating wrong answer choices takes longer. Plus, going through the process of eliminating answer choices can actually help jog your memory.

**Summary**: Start the guessing process as soon as you decide that you can't answer the question based on your knowledge.

## How to Narrow Down the Choices

The next chapter in this book (**Test-Taking Strategies**) includes a wide range of strategies for how to approach questions and how to look for answer choices to eliminate. You will definitely want to read those carefully, practice them, and figure out which ones work best for you. Here though, we're going to address a mindset rather than a particular strategy.

Your odds of guessing an answer correctly depend on how many options you are choosing from.

| Number of options left | 5 | 4 | 3 | 2 | 1 |
|---|---|---|---|---|---|
| Odds of guessing correctly | 20% | 25% | 33% | 50% | 100% |

You can see from this chart just how valuable it is to be able to eliminate incorrect answers and make an educated guess, but there are two things that many test takers do that cause them to miss out on the benefits of guessing:

- Accidentally eliminating the correct answer
- Selecting an answer based on an impression

We'll look at the first one here, and the second one in the next section.

To avoid accidentally eliminating the correct answer, we recommend a thought exercise called **the $5 challenge**. In this challenge, you only eliminate an answer choice from contention if you are willing to bet $5 on it being wrong. Why $5? Five dollars is a small but not insignificant amount of money. It's an amount you could afford to lose but wouldn't want to throw away. And while losing $5 once might not hurt too much, doing it twenty times will set you back $100. In the same way, each small decision you make—eliminating a choice here, guessing on a question there—won't by itself impact your score very much, but when you put them all together, they can make a big difference. By holding each answer choice elimination decision to a higher standard, you can reduce the risk of accidentally eliminating the correct answer.

The $5 challenge can also be applied in a positive sense: If you are willing to bet $5 that an answer choice *is* correct, go ahead and mark it as correct.

**Summary**: Only eliminate an answer choice if you are willing to bet $5 that it is wrong.

## Which Answer to Choose

You're taking the test. You've run into a hard question and decided you'll have to guess. You've eliminated all the answer choices you're willing to bet $5 on. Now you have to pick an answer. Why do we even need to talk about this? Why can't you just pick whichever one you feel like when the time comes?

The answer to these questions is that if you don't come into the test with a plan, you'll rely on your impression to select an answer choice, and if you do that, you risk falling into a trap. The test writers know that everyone who takes their test will be guessing on some of the questions, so they intentionally write wrong answer choices to seem plausible. You still have to pick an answer though, and if the wrong answer choices are designed to look right, how can you ever be sure that you're not falling for their trap? The best solution we've found to this dilemma is to take the decision out of your hands entirely. Here is the process we recommend:

**Once you've eliminated any choices that you are confident (willing to bet $5) are wrong, select the first remaining choice as your answer.**

Whether you choose to select the first remaining choice, the second, or the last, the important thing is that you use some preselected standard. Using this approach guarantees that you will not be enticed into selecting an answer choice that looks right, because you are not basing your decision on how the answer choices look.

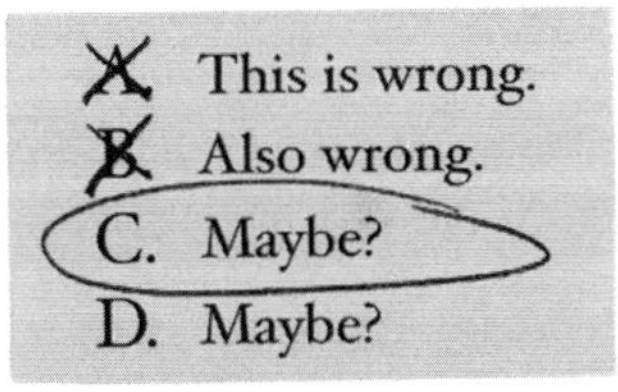


This is not meant to make you question your knowledge. Instead, it is to help you recognize the difference between your knowledge and your impressions. There's a huge difference between thinking an answer is right because of what you know, and thinking an answer is right because it looks or sounds like it should be right.

**Summary**: To ensure that your selection is appropriately random, make a predetermined selection from among all answer choices you have not eliminated.

# Test-Taking Strategies

This section contains a list of test-taking strategies that you may find helpful as you work through the test. By taking what you know and applying logical thought, you can maximize your chances of answering any question correctly!

It is very important to realize that every question is different and every person is different: no single strategy will work on every question, and no single strategy will work for every person. That's why we've included all of them here, so you can try them out and determine which ones work best for different types of questions and which ones work best for you.

## Question Strategies

### ⊘ Read Carefully

Read the question and the answer choices carefully. Don't miss the question because you misread the terms. You have plenty of time to read each question thoroughly and make sure you understand what is being asked. Yet a happy medium must be attained, so don't waste too much time. You must read carefully and efficiently.

### ⊘ Contextual Clues

Look for contextual clues. If the question includes a word you are not familiar with, look at the immediate context for some indication of what the word might mean. Contextual clues can often give you all the information you need to decipher the meaning of an unfamiliar word. Even if you can't determine the meaning, you may be able to narrow down the possibilities enough to make a solid guess at the answer to the question.

### ⊘ Prefixes

If you're having trouble with a word in the question or answer choices, try dissecting it. Take advantage of every clue that the word might include. Prefixes can be a huge help. Usually, they allow you to determine a basic meaning. *Pre-* means before, *post-* means after, *pro-* is positive, *de-* is negative. From prefixes, you can get an idea of the general meaning of the word and try to put it into context.

### ⊘ Hedge Words

Watch out for critical hedge words, such as *likely, may, can, often, almost, mostly, usually, generally, rarely*, and *sometimes*. Question writers insert these hedge phrases to cover every possibility. Often an answer choice will be wrong simply because it leaves no room for exception. Be on guard for answer choices that have definitive words such as *exactly* and *always*.

### ⊘ Switchback Words

Stay alert for *switchbacks*. These are the words and phrases frequently used to alert you to shifts in thought. The most common switchback words are *but, although*, and *however*. Others include *nevertheless, on the other hand, even though, while, in spite of, despite*, and *regardless of*. Switchback words are important to catch because they can change the direction of the question or an answer choice.

### ⊘ Face Value

When in doubt, use common sense. Accept the situation in the problem at face value. Don't read too much into it. These problems will not require you to make wild assumptions. If you have to go beyond creativity and warp time or space in order to have an answer choice fit the question, then you should move on and consider the other answer choices. These are normal problems rooted in reality. The applicable relationship or explanation may not be readily apparent, but it is there for you to figure out. Use your common sense to interpret anything that isn't clear.

## Answer Choice Strategies

### ⊘ Answer Selection

The most thorough way to pick an answer choice is to identify and eliminate wrong answers until only one is left, then confirm it is the correct answer. Sometimes an answer choice may immediately seem right, but be careful. The test writers will usually put more than one reasonable answer choice on each question, so take a second to read all of them and make sure that the other choices are not equally obvious. As long as you have time left, it is better to read every answer choice than to pick the first one that looks right without checking the others.

### ⊘ Answer Choice Families

An answer choice family consists of two (in rare cases, three) answer choices that are very similar in construction and cannot all be true at the same time. If you see two answer choices that are direct opposites or parallels, one of them is usually the correct answer. For instance, if one answer choice says that quantity $x$ increases and another either says that quantity $x$ decreases (opposite) or says that quantity $y$ increases (parallel), then those answer choices would fall into the same family. An answer choice that doesn't match the construction of the answer choice family is more likely to be incorrect. Most questions will not have answer choice families, but when they do appear, you should be prepared to recognize them.

### ⊘ Eliminate Answers

Eliminate answer choices as soon as you realize they are wrong, but make sure you consider all possibilities. If you are eliminating answer choices and realize that the last one you are left with is also wrong, don't panic. Start over and consider each choice again. There may be something you missed the first time that you will realize on the second pass.

### ⊘ Avoid Fact Traps

Don't be distracted by an answer choice that is factually true but doesn't answer the question. You are looking for the choice that answers the question. Stay focused on what the question is asking for so you don't accidentally pick an answer that is true but incorrect. Always go back to the question and make sure the answer choice you've selected actually answers the question and is not merely a true statement.

### ⊘ Extreme Statements

In general, you should avoid answers that put forth extreme actions as standard practice or proclaim controversial ideas as established fact. An answer choice that states the "process should be used in certain situations, if..." is much more likely to be correct than one that states the "process should be discontinued completely." The first is a calm rational statement and doesn't even make a definitive, uncompromising stance, using a hedge word *if* to provide wiggle room, whereas the second choice is far more extreme.

### ⊘ Benchmark

As you read through the answer choices and you come across one that seems to answer the question well, mentally select that answer choice. This is not your final answer, but it's the one that will help you evaluate the other answer choices. The one that you selected is your benchmark or standard for judging each of the other answer choices. Every other answer choice must be compared to your benchmark. That choice is correct until proven otherwise by another answer choice beating it. If you find a better answer, then that one becomes your new benchmark. Once you've decided that no other choice answers the question as well as your benchmark, you have your final answer.

### ⊘ Predict the Answer

Before you even start looking at the answer choices, it is often best to try to predict the answer. When you come up with the answer on your own, it is easier to avoid distractions and traps because you will know exactly what to look for. The right answer choice is unlikely to be word-for-word what you came up with, but it should be a close match. Even if you are confident that you have the right answer, you should still take the time to read each option before moving on.

## General Strategies

### ⊘ Tough Questions

If you are stumped on a problem or it appears too hard or too difficult, don't waste time. Move on! Remember though, if you can quickly check for obviously incorrect answer choices, your chances of guessing correctly are greatly improved. Before you completely give up, at least try to knock out a couple of possible answers. Eliminate what you can and then guess at the remaining answer choices before moving on.

### ⊘ Check Your Work

Since you will probably not know every term listed and the answer to every question, it is important that you get credit for the ones that you do know. Don't miss any questions through careless mistakes. If at all possible, try to take a second to look back over your answer selection and make sure you've selected the correct answer choice and haven't made a costly careless mistake (such as marking an answer choice that you didn't mean to mark). This quick double check should more than pay for itself in caught mistakes for the time it costs.

### ⊘ Pace Yourself

It's easy to be overwhelmed when you're looking at a page full of questions; your mind is confused and full of random thoughts, and the clock is ticking down faster than you would like. Calm down and maintain the pace that you have set for yourself. Especially as you get down to the last few minutes of the test, don't let the small numbers on the clock make you panic. As long as you are on track by monitoring your pace, you are guaranteed to have time for each question.

### ⊘ Don't Rush

It is very easy to make errors when you are in a hurry. Maintaining a fast pace in answering questions is pointless if it makes you miss questions that you would have gotten right otherwise. Test writers like to include distracting information and wrong answers that seem right. Taking a little extra time to avoid careless mistakes can make all the difference in your test score. Find a pace that allows you to be confident in the answers that you select.

### ☑ Keep Moving

Panicking will not help you pass the test, so do your best to stay calm and keep moving. Taking deep breaths and going through the answer elimination steps you practiced can help to break through a stress barrier and keep your pace.

## Final Notes

The combination of a solid foundation of content knowledge and the confidence that comes from practicing your plan for applying that knowledge is the key to maximizing your performance on test day. As your foundation of content knowledge is built up and strengthened, you'll find that the strategies included in this chapter become more and more effective in helping you quickly sift through the distractions and traps of the test to isolate the correct answer.

Now that you're preparing to move forward into the test content chapters of this book, be sure to keep your goal in mind. As you read, think about how you will be able to apply this information on the test. If you've already seen sample questions for the test and you have an idea of the question format and style, try to come up with questions of your own that you can answer based on what you're reading. This will give you valuable practice applying your knowledge in the same ways you can expect to on test day.

**Good luck and good studying!**

# Information and Data Collection

## Obtaining Company Financial Information

A good research analyst is one that takes the time to understand key financial information. At the onset, the analyst should understand the financial status of the company they are following. Are they making money? Are they paying their bills on time? Is shareholder equity increasing in line with comparable companies in the industry? The analyst should also have a good understanding of the company structure. Who are the key people within the organization? What do their employment contracts look like? How does the company make money? What are the key components to their ability to turn revenues into profit margin? The analyst should also have a good understanding of the anticipated growth for both the industry and the company. Growth is typically measured in the form of market capitalization (outstanding shares multiplied by price) and market share. In other words, given the valuation of the company's stock, how much of the overall industry do they make up? Is there room to grow without acquiring the customers of a competitor? Does a future merger or acquisition seem likely?

## Financial Statements

Form 10-K is an annual filing that is required to be submitted within 60 days (depending on filer status) of the end of a company's fiscal year. This filing is typically very detailed, containing both organizational information (such as current structure) and financial information (outstanding shares, underlying holdings, earnings, etc.). Form 10K provides much information that can be used by a research analyst's reports. Form 10-Q is a quarterly filing that is required to be submitted within 40 days (depending on filer status) of the end of the first three fiscal quarters. This form provides an up-to-date disclosure of the company's performance. While these forms do report information that is of utmost importance, there are fewer overall details than one would find in the 10-K.

## Income Statement

An income statement is used to indicate how a company performed over a specific accounting time period. The performance is broken down into operating and non-operating activities. The income statement is also known as a profit and loss statement. The operating activities section only includes revenues and expenses that are a direct result of normal business operations. The expenses include cost of goods sold, selling, general and administrative expenses, and depreciation (includes depletion and amortization). The non-operating activities section is used to report revenues and expenses related to items that are not tied to the company's normal business operations. For example, if an organization purchased a warehouse to hold its goods and sold off the equipment that was contained in the warehouse at the time of possession, this revenue would be considered non-operating.

## Balance Statement

A balance sheet is considered a snapshot of the company's net worth or financial condition. It is analyzed to determine if the company has a capital surplus or a deficit. The report is broken down into three sections: assets, liabilities, and stockholder's equity. The assets section contains current assets such as cash, accounts receivable, prepaid items, and inventory; depreciable assets such as property, buildings, and equipment; and intangible assets such as good will and trade names. The liabilities section contains current liabilities like interest due on notes, accounts payable, taxes that are owed in the short term, and unearned revenues. It also has long-term liabilities like bonds payable and long-term loans. The stockholder's equity section is the sum of common stock and retained earnings less any treasury stock.

## Cash Flow Statement

A cash flow statement is created by taking specific information from the balance sheet and the income statement to determine how the company is running from an operations perspective, including where money is coming from and how it is being spent. The statement is broken down into three sections: operations, investing, and financing. The operations section provides details as to how much cash is brought in directly from sales of a company's goods or services. The investing section details changes in cash position as a result of buying or selling equipment or other hard assets. The financing section details changes in debt and dividends.

## Various Levels of Management and Their Roles

The CEO (chief executive officer) is the highest ranking executive officer within a company. They are responsible for making high-level decisions about the future of the company and then meeting with other senior officers to dole out duties and tasks related to implementing the decision. Many times the CEO is the president of the board as well. In other cases, the CEO has a seat on the board, but the role of president is held by another. The board of directors has a responsibility to the shareholders. They are tasked to increase profits that flow through to shareholder's equity. They all have expertise in some meaningful way that can contribute to voting on actions that the CEO would like to take. The CEO answers to the board. The CFO (chief financial officer) is responsible for ensuring the company only takes on appropriate financial risks. This individual is also responsible for developing the overall financial plan for the company, and signs all official company financial statements. The COO (chief operating officer) is the individual who is responsible for overseeing the company's operations. They keep an eye on the activities performed by the company's workforce and report it to the CEO.

When a research analyst begins covering a new company, part of his or her role will be to have a good understanding of the inner workings of the company. The C-suite (CEO, COO, CFO) and the board of directors will allow the analyst to visit their facilities and meet with employees. Generally, the analyst will make several trips to the corporate headquarters to meet with top executives. Next, the analyst will make several trips to the facilities in which the products are made and/or offices that support the services provided. In addition, the analyst will be given access to the sales people, both inside sales and outside sales. This will enable the analyst to get a good sense of the caliber of the sales force and a good understanding of how the sales force differentiates the goods and services. Lastly, but certainly not least important, the analyst will meet with production employees. This could be those who work on assembly lines creating the goods sold, the production line who packages the items, or support teams who provide support for the services provided.

## Contacts in the Industry

There are several contacts that a research analyst ought to have for any company they report on. A supplier within the industry is a good place to start. As a supplier's cost of goods increases, they have little choice but to pass that increased cost along to their customers. Generally, if the cost for one supplier increases, it can be assumed that the expense will be increasing to all suppliers within that area. By maintaining a relationship with a supplier, a research analyst can get a better understanding of potential increases (or decreases) to a company's inventory and supply chain management before the financial reports are released. This can also provide some helpful information as to whether the company is meeting their financial responsibilities on a timely basis. It is also helpful for a research analyst to have contacts with the buyers. This way, if buyers are either increasing their demand for a product, or choosing to make their purchases from a competitor, the research analyst has some current knowledge of the changes, and can use that information as part of his or her overall recommendation.

There are several contacts that a research analyst ought to have related to the company they report on. Industry associations are a great place to learn about trends within an industry, as well as learn about upcoming conferences and trade shows that are worthwhile. Industry associations generally have newsletters that are printed on a semi-regular basis and can provide meaningful information for a research analyst. A research analyst should also have contacts with the competitors. It is important to keep a pulse on not just the company the analyst is following, but their main competitors as well. This is especially true in industries that are highly regulated or require following intense compliance rules. Another group of individuals that a research analyst should have relationships with are industry experts or consultants. These types of individuals are very helpful as it relates to asking general questions, hearing news that is circulating the industry, and getting a better understanding of how companies are performing within the sector.

Research analysts have many tools they can use to collect data. A few of the most common ones include attending conferences and trade shows, reading publications, analyzing financial reports, interviewing subjects, and creating and disseminating written surveys. Regardless of which techniques the analyst chooses to use, data integrity is of the utmost importance. The reports a research analyst puts together are only as good as the information they gather and analyze. In addition, research analysts must adhere to a particularly high code of conduct. Over the past few years, there has been a lot of talk about data mining and buying demographic data from those who gather it through less-than-ethical means. Research analysts should know where the data they are obtaining came from, as they are liable for the reports that utilize the information.

## Obtaining Industry Data

Part of a research analyst's job is to obtain data to use in their research reports as well as industry reports. There are a quite a few ways in which an analyst may obtain this information. One of the ways is to attend conferences, seminars, or trade shows hosted by either an entire industry or a few key players within an industry. While in attendance, the analyst has an opportunity to pick up literature from a variety of kiosks, go to presentations where new topics and trends are discussed and analyzed, hear breaking news about the industry (such as potential mergers), and any other factors that might change the earnings predictions for an upcoming quarter.

There are additional ways of obtaining industry specific information, including telephone surveys, written surveys, and web-based surveys. Telephone surveys used to be the most popular way of obtaining current thoughts on an industry or a company within the industry; however, as cell phones have replaced the need for a home phone, these types of surveys are not nearly as popular or effective. The second type of survey is a written one. These can be mail-based surveys, such as the ones sent to a new car owner after a recent purchase, or they can be seemingly impromptu surveys, such as the ones that take place at a mall or other large gatherings of people. Web-based surveys have become more common over the past 10 years. There are web sites that are solely dedicated to the taking of surveys, in exchange for points that can be used to purchase discounted items, or occasionally can be turned in for cash. Web-based surveys are helpful in that they can be used to cast a wide net in terms of diversity, or can be used to narrow down the focus to a group with a certain set of common characteristics.

Nearly every type of industry has a variety of written literature that can be utilized to gather industry information. Trade magazines, journals, and industry-specific databases are examples of this. The research analyst should gain an understanding of how each magazine or journal is respected by industry professionals, as not all are created equally. For example, some journals are used specifically for peer review, which means that a lot of research has been conducted, but the actual study and conclusion are being presented in the hopes of receiving peer feedback. Others are meant more for public consumption and therefore have a lot of advertisements contained within them. All of these publications are helpful in that they provide information about the industry and the companies within it; however, some of the publications are considered more academic in nature than others. Industry-specific databases can be used for a variety of information, including collecting demographic information, finding articles on particular subject matters, and locating contacts to interview.

### COLLECTING ECONOMIC INDICATOR DATA

There are a variety of economic indicators that research analysts analyze as part of their normal job function. A few of the more common ones include:

1. Real GDP: this is found in a report produced by the US Department of Commerce's Bureau of Economic Analysis. That report is published quarterly.
2. Money supply: this is published by the Board of Governors of the Federal Reserve System on the fourth Tuesday of every month.
3. Consumer price index: this is published by the US Department of Labor's Bureau of Labor Statistics on either a monthly basis (for three large metropolitan areas) or every other month (for all other metropolitan areas).
4. Producer price index: this is published by the US Department of Labor's Bureau of Labor Statistics on a monthly basis.
5. Consumer confidence survey: this is published by the Conference Board's Consumer Research Center on a monthly basis.
6. Unemployment statistics: these are published by the US Department of Labor's Bureau of Labor of Statistics the first Friday following the end of the previous reference month.

### GOVERNMENT STATISTICS

#### *CONSUMER CONFIDENCE*

Consumer confidence is a survey that is done on a monthly basis at the Conference Board's Consumer Research Center. In essence, the Center asks 5,000 random individuals five questions to ascertain their feelings about how the economy is doing from the perspective of the labor market, consumer spending, and general economic growth. The answers to each question will be classified as either positive, negative, or neutral. The past has shown that the answers to these questions are a good indicator of whether consumers will be spending more or less in the future.

#### *DISPOSABLE INCOME*

Disposable income is calculated by taking a household's personal income and subtracting their personal income tax payments. This leaves you with the amount they have to either save or spend. If this equation results in a negative amount, it indicates that consumers will have to use their savings to pay for their current bills.

#### *GROSS DOMESTIC PRODUCT (GDP)*

Gross domestic product is the market value of all finished goods and services produced by a country during the specific referenced time period, adjusted to take into consideration the changes in prices. In the United States, GDP is published quarterly. This is an indicator of how quickly an economy is growing as it can be compared to the data from the previous quarters as well as the data available from other countries.

### *Inflation and Interest Rates*

There is a link between inflation and interest rates. The Federal Reserve has a target inflation rate of two percent. Inflation is defined as a rise in the price of goods and services. The Federal Reserve takes current inflation rates into consideration when setting the federal funds rate, as this translates into how cheap or expensive it is for the average consumer to borrow money.

### *Unemployment Rates*

Unemployment rates are published by the US Department of Labor's Bureau of Labor Statistics on a monthly basis. This rate indicates how many new jobs were created during the previous month as compared to the number of people who were actively seeking employment. It can be further broken down to look at the particular sectors or industries that are either gaining or losing jobs.

## FINRA Rule 5130

FINRA Rule 5130 restricts members from selling new issues to accounts in which restricted persons have a beneficial interest and requires members to have procedures to ensure compliance. There are a few exemptions to this rule including the following:

1. Investment company registered under the Investment Company Act
2. Common trust fund with at least 1,000 or more accounts
3. Insurance company
4. ERISA accounts (most retirement accounts fall under this category)
5. State or municipal government benefit plans
6. 501C(3) accounts
7. Church plans

# Analysis, Modeling, and Valuation

## Economic Drivers That Impact an Industry

There are a lot of economic drivers that can be analyzed; however, the best analysts identify a few key drivers for the industry in question and do an in-depth analysis of those. For example, a few of the key ones include:

1. Analysts like to see stability in a company's offerings. If a company is considering introducing a good or service that is not in keeping with their stated mission or objective, this could be a red flag. On the flip side, a company that has only one product in their line when other competitors are consistently coming to the table with add-ons may also be a red flag.
2. Is there key legislation at either the federal or state level that would impact the company? Sometimes this can be healthy legislation, which will loosen restrictions that have impacted the industry for a long time. Other times, new legislation will restrict a company's ability to continue running their business in the same way.
3. Any time a company is seeking financing, an analyst should be asking a few questions. What is the purpose of the financing? Is it to expand operations? Support current ones? Additionally, the rate at which the financing is made available is an important question. Are banks willing to offer money at going rate or is the company's credit rating negative?

## Regression Analysis

A regression analysis is a way of determining to what degree there is a correlation between variables. This is an important concept, as it allows a research analyst to determine whether two factors actually are related to one another. For example, an analyst would be able to determine the correlation between a change in interest rates and a company's profit margin. In other words, assuming that all other factors on an income statement remained the same, would a change in the going interest rate lead to the same level of profit, an increase, or a decrease? When doing correlation studies such as a regression analysis, a statistician must be sure they are analyzing enough data, or else they may come to an incorrect conclusion. For example, if someone analyzed the 2008 recession in a vacuum (i.e., not looking at data from other years, or from prior recessions), they might come to the conclusion that stocks and bonds move in the same direction.

## Secular Trends

Secular means a long-term time frame. For most industries, this implies a period of at least 10 years. The trends that are seen when someone analyzes an industry over this duration may be different than the ones seen over a much shorter period of time. Using the stock market as an example, over a 30-year time period, the average rate of return for a diversified portfolio with moderate risk is between seven and eight percent. That is a secular trend. When the same portfolio is analyzed over shorter periods of time, much larger swings are seen. For example, if someone looked at 10 years of data, they might see that the first, sixth, ninth, and 10$^{th}$ years produced large positive returns; while the second and fourth years ended with no gain or loss; and the third, fifth, seventh, and eighth years produced negative returns. No single year may have an eight percent return, however when the entire time period is analyzed, a secular trend of an eight percent return is seen.

## Cyclical Trends

Cyclical trends are common with an industry. Cyclical returns can be looked at from a couple of different perspectives. Sometimes, the trend may be that every third quarter, there is a dip in revenue. For example, the travel industry may find that a correlation exists between school going back in session and a reduction in an opportunity to take vacations. From this regard, an analyst would know that the decline in travel during the third quarter was a normal part of the business cycle. Another way to look at cyclical trends is to say that whenever "x" occurs, the business can anticipate "y" to happen as a result. An example might be when Farmers' Almanac predicts a particularly cold and wet winter season, there is an increase in the sale of snow shovels. And as a result, when an analyst knows what the anticipated weather patterns are, they can more accurately predict sales.

## Supply and Demand

Supply and demand are usually in flux. In general, many people think that there is a one-for-one correlation between the two, meaning that a company decides how much of a product to make based on the underlying demand. And while this certainly is a large factor, it is far from the only one. Here are a few other factors that are involved in supply and demand:

1. Financial performance: do past company sales validate the idea of creating additional inventory? What is the average inventory turnover time?
2. Legal and regulatory issues: changes in the legal atmosphere as well as pending regulations can have a large impact on supply and demand calculations. For example, the loss of a patent may introduce additional competition into the market, driving down prices.
3. Cash on hand: can the company afford to pre-pay to make inventory for a predicted increase in demand? A company may know that increased demand is likely, but not be able to meet it because they do not have enough cash on hand or ability to take out additional loans.

## Competition Within an Industry

There are a number of factors that create competition within an industry. The most common ones include:

1. Financial costs: how much financial outlay is required to start up the business?
2. Expertise: is there specific expertise that must be obtained? How easy is it to meet the education or experience requirements?
3. Regulations: are there key regulations that serve to hinder competition from entering the industry? Are there patents or other legal protections that would make it difficult for competition?
4. Supply and demand: how many competitors are currently in business? How many potential customers exist?
5. Age of industry: How young is the industry? Is future growth predicted? In general, if the foremost burdens are light and the anticipated rewards are plentiful, an industry can anticipate many competitors.

## Comparative Analysis of Two Companies in the Same Industry

Sometimes the best way for an analyst to see how a particular company is performing is to compare it to another company within the industry. This enables the analyst to put some of the key metrics, ratios, and financials into perspective. For example, suppose the company that an analyst is reviewing has bad debt write offs of three percent. Without knowing how another equally-sized company in the same industry fares in this same category, the number is not really explainable. In addition, this analysis allows an analyst to see other commonalities between two companies. For example, do they use the same suppliers? Is the financing more attractive for one over the other? Do they market to the same demographics? Are their budgets for certain expense lines in keeping with one another? This allows the analyst to put the company he or she is reporting on into more context.

## Inter-Relationships of Peripheral Companies and Sectors

The term "peripheral" means not relating to the most important part of something. Therefore, a peripheral company is one that creates something that is related to someone else's business or industry and may actually be dependent on them, but is not considered a direct competitor. To put this in a very simple example, Company A may be an ice cream manufacturer. Their core line is selling half-gallons of ice cream to grocery stores throughout America. Company B may be a peripheral company that creates ice cream cones. The ice cream company may sell their own brand of ice cream cones as well, but it is considered a complimentary business line, and their profit margins are much higher on the actual ice cream sales. That being said, from the ice cream cone maker's perspective, their business is completely reliant upon ice cream sales. If people are not buying ice cream, in all likelihood, they are not buying ice cream cones either.

## Inter-Industry and Intra-Industry Competition

Inter-industry trade involves products and services that belong to different industries. Intra-industry trade, on the other hand, involves products that belong to the same industry. To avoid trying to take market share from one another, one of the goals of intra-industry competition is to increase the variety of products within the same industry. Intra-industry competition can also lead to new innovations in the way things are made, which brings down the cost. It also can lead to new features for products that have been in existence for a number of years. This product range can be highly differentiated, allowing the companies to have distinct competitive advantages.

## Divestiture

A divestiture is either the partial or full disposal of a company or a business unit via sale, exchange, closure, or bankruptcy. A divestiture can occur as a result of management making the decision to no longer operate a particular business unit, or that it was dissolved as part of a corporate bankruptcy. It can also occur when a company chooses to close just one particular warehouse, sales operation facility, or other company holding. A divestiture can occur either with the assets contained within the facility or they can sell the assets separately. Alternatively, they could transfer the assets to another work site.

## Government Regulation, Economic Policy, and Monetary Policy

Changes in government regulation, economic policy, and monetary policy have both short term and long term impacts on an industry. From a short term perspective, all changes initially translate into additional expenses for a company. Even if long term, the changes are ultimately positive for the company; initially change means more money spent on attorneys, policy reviews, systems to ensure the changes are appropriately reported, and employee training costs. Consider monetary change policies as an example. When the Federal Reserve makes a change to interest rates, it can have an immediate impact for an industry. For example, if interest rates increase, all short term debts (such as accounts payable) will be immediately impacted, and companies may try to pay these off faster to avoid the additional expense. Additionally, if the companies within a specific industry are considering issuing new debt to raise capital, they may need to increase their coupon rate, which translates into a greater interest expense to the company.

## Projections

Part of research analysts' roles requires them to be able to project the future direction for a particular industry. This can be a difficult task because so many different things factor into this projection. To begin with, a detailed look at historical and current trends is necessary. As an example, if one were to look at the banking industry over the past 10 years, they would see an industry in crisis—bailouts, cash reserve changes, additional regulation, bankruptcies, major policy changes, and ultimately instability in profitability. All of these facts would be taken into consideration to see how they will continue to impact the industry as a whole. A look at the more recent trends shows that banks are using the past events to develop greater compliance and risk management policies, are spending more capital on cybersecurity projects, and are continuing to develop new and better features to entice new customers. All of these involve additional cash outlays but (with any luck) will bring in new accounts, meaning more revenues, which would translate into additional profitability.

## Record of a Company's Financial Performance

A company's financial performance is used for a variety of reasons, and therefore ensuring it is accurately recorded is an extremely important task. One of the ways this information is used is in calculating gains and losses. One of the questions an investor will ask is how much did I earn during the period in which I held this asset? What they are asking is, relative to other assets I could have purchased, did I invest wisely? Without having the ability to analyze financial performance of similar companies over that same time period, this question cannot be answered. Another way this information is utilized deals with predicting future performance. Many analysts and investors use historical performance as an indicator of likely future performance. Therefore, preserving this information is necessary.

In many cases, historical performance is an indicator of future earnings. That is because both the economy and industries in general are cyclical in nature. Therefore, given a long enough period of time to analyze, the closer one can get at accurately predicting performance. Startup companies are harder to predict future earnings for because the period of time one can analyze is relatively short. However, if economic conditions remain stable, an analyst could use sales growth predictions as a means of projecting future revenue streams and ultimately profits. When a company has a longer historical record, predicting future earnings can be a little more accurate because it is easier to find a period of time that is a reasonable depiction of current economic and market conditions.

## Fundamental Analysis

Fundamental analysis is a means of determining a company's intrinsic value. To calculate this value, an economist or analyst would look at economic data, financial returns, and qualitative and quantitative data, all in an attempt to look at all the different things that factor into the valuation of a security. Once all of this information is analyzed and a valuation is determined, an investor could theoretically use the valuation to determine whether the current market price is a fair one. Because there are so many different factors that influence the valuation of a security, there are many ways in which fundamental analysis can be approached. Fundamental analysis is an ongoing valuation method because the inputs are constantly in flux.

## Growth and Profits

There are a number of factors that influence a company's growth and profits. In general, for a company to grow, they must expand or improve upon their operations in some meaningful way. That requires capital. Capital can be achieved through issuing new debt or additional equity. A company's ability to issue new bonds requires a good credit rating, low interest rates, and a steady revenue stream to pay the interest and ultimately the principal due on the bonds. To issue additional equity, the company needs an investment bank that is willing to provide favorable terms, a strong market in which to sell the offerings, and the ability to ensure that outstanding equity will not be diluted by the new issuance. Once additional capital is received, a company requires a favorable environment in which to operate—low turnover and high retention, productive workers, low taxes, lack of competition, and regulatory compliance that is easy to comply with. If any one of these factors is not present, it will be difficult to grow.

## Generally Accepted Accounting Principles and the Financial Accounting Standards Board

Generally Accepted Accounting Principles (GAAP) is an internationally accepted set of accounting principles that can be incorporated in any company, locality, or country that follow the guidelines. The organization tries to impart fairness, particularly in an investor's ability to trust that a company or government's financial statements are put together using the same set of underlying rules and principles. The Financial Accounting Standards Board (FASB) is a non-profit organization based out of the United States which helps ensure that Generally Accepted Accounting Principles (GAAP) are implemented and strictly followed by all public companies in the United States.

## Corporate Governance

Corporate governance is the way in which a company is run. It includes the many stakeholders of a company—its board of directors, executive management team, officers, employees, customers, stockholders, vendors, financiers, and the community at large. Basically, anyone who stands to gain or lose something as a result of the company is part of the corporate governance structure. The policies and procedures effectuated by the company, whether the company separates the chairman and the CEO roles, whether there is visibility and transparency around decisions and compensation, whether employees know the financial stability of the company—all of these are part of the term corporate governance.

## Qualitative and Quantitative Data

Quantitative data is the kind that most people automatically think of when the word "data" comes to mind. These are data that can be measured, including monetary value, financial metrics, age of assets, statistics, number of items, or number of employees. Qualitative data is information that is not numerically based. Things like the talent possessed by an employee, general observations, or gender would all fall under qualitative data. A research analyst uses both types of data when compiling information necessary to create their reports. For example, interviews with production employees would be a qualitative data collection technique, while the number of production employees on site would be quantitative.

## Ratios and Metrics

There are a number of key ratios and metrics that investors and analysts use to value a company and determine whether investment in the company makes sense. The majority of the data necessary to compile these statistics comes straight from the company's financial statements (cash flow, income statement, net worth, and general annual report). Therefore, to the extent that a company's financial statements are not created following all accepted accounting principles or are not audited properly to ensure a high degree of integrity, key ratios could potentially be calculated using faulty data and lead to inaccurate results.

## Calculations and Ratios That Are Used in the Valuation of a Company

### *Cost of Capital*

Cost of capital is the total cost of the all funds used to finance an organization. It takes into consideration both equity and debt financing. Calculating this is a multiple step process:

- Step 1: The formula for the cost of debt financing is: Yield to Maturity of Debt x (1 – T), where T is the company's marginal tax rate.
- Step 2: The formula for the cost of equity financing is found using the capital asset pricing model (CAPM) and therefore is: Risk - Free Rate of Return + (The Company's Beta x Risk Premium)
- Step 3: Determine the ratio of debt to total financing, and equity to total financing
- Step 4: Multiply each ratio by its respective cost

### *Discounted Cash Flow*

Discounted cash flow is a valuation method that determines how attractive an investment opportunity is. It uses future cash flow projections and discounts them back to present value. If the calculation results in an amount that is higher than the cost of the investment, then it might make sense to go forward with the investment.

### *Discounted Cash Flow and Dividend Discount Method*

The dividend discount model is one that values the price of a particular stock by using the expected future dividends and discounting them back to find the present value. An investor would use the result to determine whether the stock is undervalued or overvalued.

The formula is: $\frac{Dividend\ per\ share}{Discount\ Rate - Dividend\ Growth\ Rate}$

### *Dividend Yield*

The dividend yield is a ratio that is used to determine how much a company pays out in the form of dividends each year in relation to the stock price.

The formula is: $\frac{Annual\ Dividends\ per\ share}{Price\ per\ share}$

### *Earnings Yield*

Earnings yield is the inverse of the P/E ratio. It illustrates the percentage of each dollar invested in the stock that was earned by the company.

The formula is: $\frac{Earnings\ per\ share}{Current\ Market\ Price}$

### *Economic Profit*

Economic profit is another name for economic value added. This is a different way to view profit, other than accounting profit. Economic profit allows you to look at what you could have done with the money, time, and space "spent" on a particular venture. In other words, it takes into consideration opportunity cost to determine whether a company gained or lost money by using its resources in a particular way.

### Enterprise Value (EV) to EBITDA

Enterprise value is a measure of a company's value. It is a quick valuation to determine starting value for a potential takeover bid that takes into consideration the debt that they would take on.

The formula is: $\frac{Market\ capitalization + Debt + Minority\ Interest + Preferred\ Shares - Total\ Cash\ and\ Cash\ Equivalents}{EBITDA}$

### Enterprise Value (EV) to Sales

Enterprise value is a measure of a company's value. It is a quick valuation to determine starting value for a potential takeover bid. When compared to the sales, it gives investors a starting point for how much it would cost to buy a company's sales.

The formula is: $\frac{Market\ capitalization + Debt + Minority\ Interest + Preferred\ Shares - Total\ Cash\ and\ Cash\ Equivalents}{Annual\ Sales}$

### Free Cash Flow Yield

Free cash flow takes into consideration account capital expenditures and other expenses necessary to keep a business operating. Free cash flow yield produces a metric that allows an investor to compare the free cash flow to the market price per share. Generally, the higher the ratio, the more attractive the investment.

Free cash flow yield equals: $\frac{Free\ Cash\ Flow\ per\ share}{Current\ Market\ Price\ per\ share}$

### Price to Book Value

Price to book value is a ratio that is used to compare the market value of a stock to its book value. It is also known as the price-equity ratio.

The formula is: $\frac{Closing\ Price\ of\ the\ Stock}{Latest\ Quarter's\ Book\ Value\ per\ share}$

### Price to Earnings (P/E)

Price to earnings is a measure of a company's current share price compared to the per-share earnings, to indicate whether investors are expecting high or low future growth. This is also known as a price multiple or an earnings multiple.

The formula is: $\frac{Market\ Value\ per\ share}{Earnings\ per\ share}$

### Price Earnings to Growth Ratio

Price to earnings to growth (PEG Ratio) is a measure of a stock's value while also considering the company's earnings growth. It allows investors to determine whether a stock is potentially undervalued.

The formula is: $\frac{Price\ to\ Earnings\ Ratio}{Annual\ EPS\ Growth}$

### *Price to Free Cash Flow*

Price to free cash flow is a way to look at the company's market price to its annual free cash flow. This calculation allows an investor to consider the fact that the company is either trying to maintain their cash flow or grow their business.

The calculation for price to free cash flow equals: $\frac{Market\ Capitalization}{Free\ Cash\ Flow}$

### *Private Equity Value of the Parts Analysis*

Private equity value of the parts analysis is used when a company is trying to decide whether it makes more sense to break up the company into different divisions and spin them off, rather than sell the company as one entity. Simply put, the company would value the amount they would receive if they sold the company whole versus how much money they would receive if they broke the company up into separate pieces.

## Undervalued vs. Overvalued Stock

An undervalued stock is one that is priced less than what it is believed to be worth. A company's worth can be determined by evaluating financial statements, P/E Ratio (price to earnings), ROA (return on assets), and retained earnings. An overvalued stock is one where the current price is not justified when compared to the company's anticipated earnings. As a result, in general, it is believed that the price will soon fall. Knowing whether a stock is undervalued vs. overvalued can help an investor make a few key decisions: do they want to buy an undervalued stock? Or consider a derivative strategy involving the overvalued security instead?

## Mergers and Acquisitions

Mergers and acquisitions can have a major impact on an industry. The degree of the impact will depend upon the number of major players within the industry and the size of the two companies that are merging. For example, in an industry with a lot of competition, the merger of two small companies may not attract attention or impact the industry as a whole in any major way. Conversely, in an industry that only has three or four key players, a merger of two of them has the ability to create upheaval in the industry. An example that may come to mind is the merger between Charter and Time Warner Cable. Both of these companies are giants in their industries; the merging of the two would allow for them to dominate the cable TV industry.

## Limitations That Are Placed on the Use of FINRA's Name

A member may state that it is a member of FINRA as long as the following conditions are met:

- When publishing a communication with the public, the communication must comply with Rule 2210. The communication must state that FINRA does not endorse, indemnify or guarantee the business practices or selling methods of the member, the class or type of securities offered or any specific security.
- For over-the-counter transactions, the confirmation must state that the transaction has been executed in conformity with the NASD Uniform Practice Code.
- If a member has a website, the member must indicate FINRA membership and include a hyperlink to FINRA's home page.

## Ranking Entity

A ranking entity is an entity that provides general information on investment companies to the public. The ranking entity is independent of the investment company and its affiliates. Investment company rankings may only be used in advertisements and sales literature if the ranking was published by a ranking entity or if the ranking is based on the performance measurements of a ranking entity. In addition, the following disclosures must be made:

- An investment company or investment company family may only be discussed as being a top performer in a category if it is ranked first in that category.
- Advertisements and sales literature must prominently disclose the name of the category, the number of investment companies in the category, the name of the ranking entity, the length of the period and its ending date and the basis for the ranking.
- That past performance is no guarantee of future performance.
- If the ranking takes loads into account for investment companies that assess front-end sales loads.
- The publisher of the ranking data.
- If the ranking consists of a symbol rather than a number, the meaning of the symbol.

## Bond Mutual Fund Volatility Rating

A bond mutual fund volatility rating is the description an independent third party gives to the sensitivity to changes in market conditions and the economy, of the net asset value of a portfolio of an open-end management investment company that invests in debt securities. This volatility rating must be based on an evaluation of objective factors, such as the credit quality of the fund's portfolio holdings, the market price volatility, the fund's performance, interest rate risk, prepayment risk and currency risk. A bond mutual fund volatility rating may only be used in sales literature when:

- The rating does not give the fund a risk rating
- The most recent rating is used and the information is current of the recent calendar quarter
- The rating must be based on objective and quantifiable factors
- The rating and the disclosure statement must be clear, concise and understandable
- The rating issuing entity must provide an explanation of the rating methodology to investors. This explanation may be made through a toll-free number or a website.

## Investment Analysis Tool

An investment analysis tool is a computer-created simulation and statistical analysis of an investment outcome. It is used to help determine the potential risks and returns of an investment choice. The outcomes can be charted to show the forecasted results of a particular investment, investment strategy or investment style. A member may provide the results generated by an investment analysis tool in written reports, advertisements and sales literature when:

- The criteria and methodology of the tool are described along with its limitations and key assumptions.
- The results that may vary are explained.
- The investments considered in the investment are stated. There must also be an explanation of how the tool selects investments, if the tool favors any securities and that other securities may be superior to those selected.

In addition, a disclosure must be made in a clear and prominent position that states that the information generated by the investment analysis tool is hypothetical, does not reflect actual investment results and is not a guarantee of future results.

## HISTORICAL PERFORMANCE DATA

Historical performance data includes records and statistics that show the performance of past recommendations or of transactions. This data may be included in security futures sales literature and correspondence under the following conditions:

- The communications is accompanied or preceded by the security futures risk disclosure statement
- The recommendation is balanced, the records and statistics are clearly listed and the data covers the past 12-month period.
- The date and price of the recommendation or transaction are included
- Commissions, fees and daily margin obligations are disclosed
- General market conditions and comparisons to market conditions are discussed
- A statement that historical performance is not an indicator of future performance
- The communication is approved by a principal qualified to supervise security futures activities

# Preparation of Research Reports

## Initiation Report

An initiation report is created when a research analyst determines that they will begin covering a particular stock. An initiation report is only utilized when the research analyst has never followed the company in the past. The report put together by the analyst will include a variety of details about both the company and the stock. This includes some general information about the company's business model, overall financial well-being, and predictions of future revenue streams and likely profits. Ultimately, the report leads up to the recommendation of whether the analyst currently recommends buying, holding, or selling the stock. Lastly, an initiation report is an indication that investors can expect periodic updates from the analyst on that company.

## Earnings Reports

Earnings reports are ones that detail the financial well-being of the company during the period under review. Generally speaking, there are ones created on a quarterly basis, with one of these being the annual earnings report. Earnings reports come out in a few different formats. The earnings preview generally comes first and is the initial indicator of a company's earnings during the relevant time period. This report won't provide much in the way of details; it is more like a sample of the larger report to come. The earnings analysis and earnings review reports provide greater details. The analysis is a breakdown of all the data used to compile the overall earnings while the earnings review provides a summary from the chairman of the board and/or CEO, detailing key factors that they would like to draw the investor's attention to. These notes often explain unexpected expenditures or economic conditions that impacted overall earnings.

## Change of Ratings

When a research analyst is covering a particular stock, it is very common for them to announce changes in their ratings or give recommendations that are in contrast to a prior report. While all reports published by analysts require thorough research, these reports require the analyst to be very confident in their ability to defend their opinions. This is especially true because reports that represent a change over previous recommendations tend to get noticed by the media and many investors make decisions as a result of the report and the recommendations within it. The report will discuss the new rating and provide details that lead to the decision, including changes in corporate structure, the company business model, the economic environment, or anticipated future earnings.

## Elimination of Coverage

When a research analyst intends to terminate coverage of a company, they are required to give advance notice and produce one final recommendation or rating first. The reason this is a requirement is to ensure that an analyst does not simply decide to terminate coverage rather than publish a negative report. However, if the reason the stock is no longer being followed is linked to the fact that the analyst has left their firm, it may not always be reasonable for a final research report to be created. In that case, the company that the analyst was affiliated with can simply disclose their final rating or recommendation and explain why they have decided to terminate coverage.

## Components of a Research Report

### Business Model Analysis

Business model analysis allows a research analyst to pick apart a company's overall business model to ultimately determine how the company plans to make money. This includes looking at their main revenue sources, their customer base, advertising philosophy, and business structure. Analyzing a business model will also allow a research analyst to determine how quickly the company will likely be able to adjust to changes in regulations or market conditions.

### Company Overview

Company overview allows a research analyst to get a good understanding of the company, its history, divisions, corporate structure, and board of directors. It allows for all the other details to be put in perspective.

### Competitive Position

Competitive position allows the research analyst to see how the company fits in with its peers. In doing this review, it becomes clear who the main competition is, who has the majority of the market share, whose position is growing or shrinking, and how the company is able to differentiate themselves from their competition.

### Dividend Outlook

Dividend outlook looks at the historical and current dividend yields as well as overall economic conditions to estimate what future dividends are likely to be. This also takes into consideration whether the company is in a growth stage and how much of the overall profits are being reinvested into the company.

### Financial Position

Financial position is a key component of a research report. It discusses the overall financial well-being of the company, what their underlying capital structure is (debt vs. equity), and looks at some key financial ratios to determine how likely the company is to continue being solvent, meet their debt obligations, and improve their bottom line profit.

### Industry Overview

Industry overview takes a look at the industry as a whole, including financial trends, key players, and market share.

### Investment Thesis

Investment thesis lays out the beliefs that the research analysts took into consideration when determining their ultimate position. This is a way to pull out the most pertinent facts, observations, and economic conditions that were given the most weight in their ultimate decision. If written well, the investment thesis will bring the average investor to the same conclusion.

### Quality of Company Management

As part of the research report, analysts provides their evaluation on the quality of company management. This includes a look at their backgrounds, level of expertise, and overall effectiveness. In general it is believed that a company is only as good as its leadership.

### Ratings of a Company

A company's credit rating is exceptionally important, as this is an indicator of whether credit agencies believe that a company will be able to make good on their debts. Investors tend to expect a higher coupon rate in exchange for riskier investments. If the company's credit rating is subpar, this will impact the company's ability to raise cash quickly and with inexpensive terms.

### Recent Company News

The reporting of recent company news is an important part of a thorough research report. This gives the public a review of all relevant news that has either been reported and has been obtained by credible, verifiable sources along with a general explanation of how that news will impact the future of the company and their revenues.

### Risk of Investment

Part of the research report is detailing all the risks that an investor might face, including market risk (overall systematic risk), default risk (non-systematic risk), inflation risk (calculate the real rate of return), and interest rate risk (particularly for investments with a longer duration).

### Valuation of Company Stock

Valuation of company stock takes into consideration whether a stock is overvalued; undervalued; or appropriately valued taking into consideration financial ratios, overall industry trends, company news, and general market conditions.

## Registered Supervisory Analyst Approval That Must Be Obtained Before Disseminating Reports

Prior to disseminating a research report, a supervisory analyst that is deemed acceptable by the Securities Exchange Commission must approve the report. It is conceivable that the supervisory analyst may not have the necessary expertise within a particular industry or sector. In that case, the approval may come from a product specialist, as designated by the firm. In the rare event that a product specialist with the appropriate expertise is not available, the report will be approved by a supervisory analyst employed by another company.

## Certification Required by the Research Analyst That Prepares a Research Report

Regulation AC requires that a research analyst or broker/dealer that publishes a research report will include a certification by the research analyst. This certification contains:

- A statement that the views expressed in the research report accurately reflect the personal views of the research analyst regarding the issuer or the issuer's securities
- A statement that the research analyst's compensation is not related to the recommendation made in the research report
- A statement that identifies the source, amount and purpose of any compensation that is related to the recommendation made by the research analyst

Broker/dealers who publish and distribute research reports prepared by third party research analysts are exempt from Regulation AC requirements.

### Trading Restrictions Associated with Publishing Research

The following trading restrictions must be followed by research analysts when a research report publication is pending:

1. Research analysts may not receive shares before the initial public offering if the issuer's principal business is the same as any subject company followed by the analyst.
2. Research analysts may not trade in any security issued by a subject company that they follow beginning 30 days before the publication of a research report involving that company and ending five days after the publication without specific consent from their legal department.
3. Research analysts may not buy or sell any security issued by a subject company they follow if the transaction would not be in keeping with the rating from their most recently published research report.

### Items That Are Not Classified as a Research Report

A research report is a written communication that includes an analysis of an issuer's securities and sufficient information to make an investment decision. The following communications are not considered research reports and are exempt from Rule 2711:

- Discussions of economic, political and market conditions
- Summaries of broad-based indices, supply and demand, trading volume and market holdings
- Notification of ratings and price changes
- Communications that are distributed to less than 15 customers
- Periodic reports that discuss the past performance of a security
- Internal communications that are not released outside the broker-dealer
- Communications that are filed as part of a registration statement

### Industry Report

An industry report is one that breaks down an industry into detailed and easy-to-digest pieces. It is a comprehensive way of studying an overall industry or sector. Some common items to see as part of an industry report include:

1. Definition of the industry: what it does and does not include
2. Names of the major businesses within that industry
3. Market share
4. Industry trends, including sales, revenues, and overall profits
5. Employment statistics, including a detailed look at the overall composition of the work force
6. Strengths, weaknesses, opportunities and threats (also known as SWOT analysis)
7. Overall outlook for the industry going forward

### Self-Regulatory Organizations

A self-regulatory organization (SRO) is a non-governmental agency that develops rules and regulations that are followed by those in the industry. Their end goal is to ensure that the industry maintains a high degree of integrity. A common one in the United States is the National Association of Securities Dealers (NASD). The NASD was formed under the Maloney Act and serves to regulate the over-the-counter market. NASD puts together a list of rules and regulations that those who are licensed must follow. Failure to comply results in suspension, revocation of license, and/or fines. The NASD also provides the basic code of conduct that brokerage firms are expected to follow. This is all to ensure that the financial marketplace is operated with integrity and honor.

### Investment Banking

The investment banking department is responsible for performing all of the investment banking services for a member broker/dealer. These investment banking services include underwriting securities issues, participating as a selling group member, providing financial advice during mergers and acquisitions and raising venture capital for start-up companies.

Research departments prepare research reports. Research reports are a means of communication with customers and the public. Research reports contain an analysis of an issuer's securities and information to facilitate an informed investment decision. To ensure objectivity and reliability, research departments are isolated from all other departments.

### Line Graphs and Price Targets

Line graphs must be used in a research report when the member broker/dealer has assigned a rating or price target to the securities of an issuer for at least one year. This line graph must:

- List the closing price of the securities for the shorter of (1) the period for which a rating or price target was assigned or (2) three years.
- Indicate the date on which each rating or price target was assigned or changed.
- Be current as of the end of the last calendar quarter.

When a research reports contains a price target, the following must be disclosed:

- The valuation methods used to determine the price target.
- The basis for the price target.
- The risk factors that may interfere in achieving the price target.

# Rules, Regulations, and Information Memos

## STANDARDS THAT APPLY TO ALL COMMUNICATIONS WITH THE PUBLIC

There are several standards that apply to all communications with the public. These standards include:

- All communications with the public must be based on the principles of fair dealing and good faith. The information contained in the communications must be fair, balanced and provide a basis for evaluating a security, industry or service. Material facts must be included in the communication so that the information is not misleading.
- Communications with the public may not include any untrue, false, exaggerated, unwarranted or misleading statements.
- Footnotes may only be used if the information contained in the footnote will not impede an investor's understanding of the information.
- Communications with the public may not predict or project future performance. It may not imply that past performance is an indication of future performance. Also, no exaggerated claims, opinions or forecasts may be made in the communication.
- If a communication contains a testimonial regarding the technical aspect of investing, the opinion must come from a person with experience with and knowledge of the topic.

## EXEMPTIONS TO THE FILING REQUIREMENTS FOR COMMUNICATIONS WITH THE PUBLIC

The following communications with the public are exempt from filing requirements and spot-check procedures:

- Advertisements and sales literature that have been previously filed and that are used without any material changes
- Advertisements and sales literature used for recruiting purposes
- Advertisements and sales literature that announce changes in a member's name, personnel, address and telephone number, ownership, offices and business structure
- Advertisements and sales literature that only identify the member or offer a security at a specific price
- Prospectuses, fund profiles and offering circulars that have been filed with the SEC or a state
- Announcements that state that a member participated in a private placement
- Press releases sent to members of the media
- Independently prepared reprints
- Correspondence
- Institutional sales material

### Disclosure Requirements

Advertisements and sales literature must comply with several disclosure requirements. When advertisements and sales literature provide testimonials regarding investment advice or investment performance, the following must be included:

- A note stating that the testimonial may not be representative of the experience of other clients
- A statement that the testimonial is not a guarantee of future performance
- If any compensation was paid for the testimonial: When there is a comparison of investments or services, the disclosure must state the material differences including the investment objectives, costs and expenses, liquidity, safety, guarantees or insurance, fluctuation of principal or return and tax features.

All advertisements and sales literature must include the following:

- The name of the member
- The relationship between the member and any non-member mentioned
- The products or services being offered by the member when names other than the member are mentioned

When communications with the public contain information on the performance data of non-money market fun open-end management investment companies, the standardized performance information required by Rule 482 of the Securities Act of 1933 and by Rule 34b-1 of the Investment Company Act of 1940 must be disclosed. The information that must be disclosed includes:

- The maximum sales charge imposed on purchases or the maximum deferred sales charge
- The total annual fund operating expense ratio, gross of any fee waivers or expense reimbursements

This information must be displayed prominently in a text box that contains only the required information. This may also include any comparative performance and fee data required by Rule 482 and rule 34b-1.

### Guidelines Used to Ensure That Communications with the Public Are Not Misleading

FINRA members must ensure that communications with the public comply with all applicable standards. The list of guidelines to which the member must conform include:

- Statements must not be misleading within the context in which they are made. One way to meet this guideline is to balance risks and potential benefits in regards to fluctuating prices, uncertainty of dividends, rates of return and yield on investment.
- The audience must be taken into consideration. The level of explanation or amount of information provided must be appropriate for the audience.
- The information must be clear to avoid misunderstanding.
- References to tax-free or tax-exempt income must state if, and what, income taxes may apply.

### Guidelines Used to Ensure That Recommendations of Securities Are Not Misleading

When a member makes a recommendation in advertisements and sales literature, there must be a basis for the recommendation and the following must be disclosed:

- If the member was making a market in the securities being recommended or was a manager of a public offering of the securities within the past 12 months.
- If the member or its officers have a financial interest in the securities being recommended and the nature of the financial interest.
- The member must offer to furnish the investment information supporting the recommendation.
- If a member refers to a past recommendation, all recommendations over the past year of the same type, grade or classification must be disclosed.

### Advertisements and Sales Literature for Variable Life Insurance and Variable Annuities

In addition to the general standards governing communications with the public, the following general guidelines are applied to advertisements and sales literature for variable life insurance policies and variable annuities:

- All communications must clearly describe the product as either a variable life insurance policy or a variable annuity. The specific name of the product may also be mentioned. The description of the product may not imply that the product or its underlying account is a mutual fund.
- Communications may not imply that variable life insurance and variable annuities are short-term, liquid investments. Any discussion of liquidity must describe the negative result of early redemptions. Any discussion of loans and withdrawals must describe the impact on cash values and death benefits.
- Any claims of guarantees must not be overemphasized or exaggerated. The communication must not represent or imply that a guarantee applies to the investment return or principal value of the separate account.
- The communication may contain historical performance in order to illustrate an existing fund's predicted performance as if it had been an investment option within a variable life insurance policy or a variable annuity. The communication may not include an existing fund's performance if it is used to promote the investment in a similar investment option.
- Comparisons may only be used if the comparison complies with Rule 2210.
- Ranking may only be used to show the performance of the separate account or the underlying investment option.
- Communications regarding a single premium variable life insurance may discuss the investment features as long as there is an explanation of the life insurance features.

### Section 11 of the Securities Act of 1933 - Civil Liabilities on Account of False Registration Statement

Section 11 of the Securities Act of 1933 lists those who can be held liable in civil court in the event that a registration statement contains an untrue statement of material information or omits key information. According to this section, the following individuals can be held liable by the purchaser of the security: anyone who signed the registration statement or was involved in the preparation (such as accountants and appraisers), the underwriter of the security, and anyone who was on the board of directors at the time of the signing. The specific damages that an investor can attempt to recoup include the following:

1. The price at which the security was offered to the public
2. The price at which the security would have been disposed of in the market prior to the filing of the law suit
3. The lesser of the price at which the security would have been disposed of in the market at the time of judgment or the difference between the amount paid for the security and the value of the security at the time of the filing of the law suit
4. In addition, at the discretion of the judge, the issuer may be required to the pay the reasonable attorney fees and court costs paid by the investor.

## Section 12 of the Securities Act of 1933 - Civil Liabilities Arising in Connection With Prospectuses and Communications

Section 12 of the Securities Act of 1933 details the liabilities that an investor can attempt to recoup in the event that a material omission or misstatement in a prospectus is found to have occurred. In civil court, the investor may potentially be awarded the full amount paid for the security in question less any amounts received at the time of disposal. In addition, this section lays out the fact that anyone who was involved in the creation of the prospectus and did not exercise reasonable caution in determining its validity can be held liable for the damages.

## Section 15 of the Securities Act of 1933 - Liability of Controlling Persons

Section 15 of the Securities Act of 1933 states that anyone who is connected via ownership, agency, or general understanding with a person held liable under Section 11 or 12 of the Act may also be held liable, unless it is clear that they had no access to information that contradicts that which was published in the registration statement and/or prospectus. In other words, this individual must be able to prove that they did not have knowledge that should have been brought forward. This section goes on to state that anyone who knowingly or recklessly provides material or significant assistance to anyone who is in violation of any provisions referenced in the Securities Act of 1933 can be held liable.

## Section 17 of the Securities Act of 1933 - Fraudulent Interstate Transactions

Section 17 of the Securities Act of 1933 states that it is unlawful for any person involved in the sale or offering of a security may not implement certain means of interstate commerce communications. Specifically referenced in this section are the following:

1. Communications intended to defraud
2. Communications intended to obtain compensation or property using untrue material facts, key omissions of information, or statements that in general are misleading
3. Communications that, if acted upon, would result in fraud or deceit

## FINRA Rule 2262 - Disclosure of Control Relationship with Issuer

FINRA Rule 2262 states that a member who controls the issuer of a security or is controlled by the issuer of a security must disclose this relationship to a customer prior to entering into a contract for the sale or purchase of the security in question. The preference is that this be disclosed in writing. However, if the member gives the disclosure verbally, a supplemental disclosure must be sent to the customer prior to transaction completion.

## FINRA Rule 1250 - Continuing Education Requirements

FINRA Rule 1250 establishes the need for continuing education for a FINRA licensed broker. Unless otherwise instructed, individuals must complete their continuing education requirements within 120 days of the second anniversary of holding their license. Failure to complete the continuing education requirements results in having one's license put into inactive status until brought up to date. The continuing education may be provided by the firm that the broker works for, provided that certain elements are in place.

This includes the following:

1. The firm has a designated principal or officer in charge
2. The delivery takes place at a site under the control of the firm
3. The continuing education is supervised by a proctor
4. The sites are made available to FINRA for examination
5. A letter of attestation is sent to the designated examining authority (DEA) detailing items 1-4 above

## FINRA 1220 - Registration of a Research Analyst

FINRA Rule 1220 lays out the requirements that must be fulfilled before someone can perform the duties of a research analyst. These requirements are as follows:

1. Register as a general securities representative
2. Pass a Qualifying Examination for Research Analysts

Upon written request, this specific requirement may be waived in the event that the individual has completed Levels I and II of the CFA Exam and only prepares technical research reports, and has continuously worked as a research analyst since completing Level II of the CFA Exam.

## FINRA Rule 5230 - Payments Involving Publications that Influence Market Price of a Security

FINRA Rule 5230 states that no one may receive anything of value in exchange for publishing something that will influence the purchase or sale of a security. This includes any publications that occur via the Internet, television, and in writing. There are specific exemptions laid out in the rule, including the following:

1. A communication that is clearly an advertisement
2. A communication that includes a disclosure of the amount of compensation received
3. A research report, as specifically defined by FINRA Rule 2241

## FINRA Rule 5141 - Sale of Securities in a Fixed Price Offering

FINRA Rule 5141 states that those affiliated with a selling syndicate, a syndicate group, or an underwriter for a fixed price offering may not sell or offer that security for less than the stated public price. This rule will remain in place until the public offering is complete or until the member firm is unable to continue selling the offering at the stated public price.

## FINRA Rule 5280 – Trading Ahead of Research Reports

FINRA Rule 5280 states that the following trading restrictions must be followed by research analysts when a research report publication is pending:

1. Research analysts may not receive shares before the initial public offering if the issuer's principal business is the same as any subject company followed by the analyst.
2. Research analysts may not trade in any security issued by a subject company that they follow beginning 30 days before the publication of a research report involving that company and ending five days after the publication without specific consent from their legal department.
3. Research analysts may not buy or sell any security issued by a subject company they follow if the transaction would not be in keeping with the rating from their most recently published research report.

## Buy-Side Analysts, Portfolio Managers, and Hedge Fund Managers

Buy-side analysts are people who make stock recommendations to member firms. They make their recommendations by reading and watching news, confirming details mentioned in reports issued by other sources, and building statistical and asset models.

Portfolio managers oversee either the entirety or a portion of an investor's asset base in exchange for a fee. They do this by making both strategic and tactical decisions, taking into consideration the investor's goals, sophistication, and risk tolerance.

Hedge fund managers use a variety of sophisticated investment strategies to maximize the return for their investors in exchange for a relatively high fee. As the minimum investment is generally very high and from a fiduciary perspective, hedge funds should only make up a small portion of an investor's overall portfolio; only high wealth investors tend to be appropriate.

## Determining Market Size, Cyclical Nature, and Growth Rate

Collecting industry data is an important part of a research analyst's role, as it provides some very useful information about the future of the industry, including the sustainability of sales growth. To begin with, it is necessary to understand how much market share the industry has already recognized. For an industry to grow, there must still be enough uncaptured market share remaining to not only continue their current revenue stream, but to add to it. This is especially true for industries that are considered luxury, disposable, or one-time purchases. The market size and market share lead to being able to calculate the anticipated growth rate. Often times published growth rates are pro forma growth rates, meaning that the industry anticipates growth that will be as much as the prior year with a standard amount added in for good measure. A research analyst's role involves deconstructing the underlying assumptions that went into the calculation to determine whether the growth rate is realistic. Another reason that industry data collection is important is that it allows the analyst to look at the cyclical trends for the industry. For example, are there specific times of year that the industry tends to slow? Or are there certain market based events that contribute to additional growth?

## Determining the Supply Curve, Customer Demand, and Regulatory Issues

Collecting industry data is an important part of a research analyst's role, as it provides some very useful information about the future of the industry, including likely future demand and supply curve details. The supply curve provides a visual of the supply and demand for the goods and services within the industry. It allows an analyst to identify trends within the industry and begin to understand what customer demand will look like going forward. Customer demand is a contributing factor to a good industry report; after all, the overall expenses for an industry may be on the decline or perhaps an industry has discovered a new distribution model, but sales revenue is the only thing that allows an industry to take advantage of these benefits, and sales are based on customer demand. Regulatory issues are also an important factor to be considered. Some industries are more heavily regulated than others. Some industries have ever-changing rules and regulations that require analyzing and outside counsel. In some cases, there is a very short period of time for the industry to adapt to the new regulations, at which point heavy fines are levied.

## Securities Act of 1933

Before the market crash of 1929, the sale of investment securities was regulated by individual state laws. The market crash of 1929 caused serious turmoil in the investment industry. This turmoil caused instability in the investment market and a lack of confidence by the investing public. These results made it clear that there were problems in the way that investment securities were regulated. The problems identified included:

- The need for more detailed disclosure by companies selling new issues of securities
- The need for uniformity in the financial statements to help investors make better investment decisions
- The need to prevent misrepresentation and fraudulent activities in the securities markets.

The purpose of the Securities Act of 1933 was to provide for uniform regulation of new issues of securities. The Securities Act of 1933 required that companies provide the Securities and Exchange Commission and investors with a prospectus and registration statement before issuing new securities.

A security can be any of a number of investment vehicles. Securities include notes, stocks, treasury stock, security futures, bonds, debentures, evidence of indebtedness, certificates of interest or participation in any profit sharing agreement, collateral trust certificates, pre-organization certificates or subscriptions, transferable shares, investment contracts, voting-trust certificates, certificates of deposit for a security, or fractional undivided interests in any mineral rights. A security can also be a put, call, straddle, option or privilege on any certificate of deposit, group or index of securities or foreign currency. A security is also the warrant or right to subscribe to or purchase any of the securities mentioned here.

## Securities and Exchange Act of 1934

The Securities and Exchange Act of 1934 was the second piece of federal legislation that was enacted to help improve the US economy after the market crash of 1929. While the Securities Act of 1933 dealt with new issues of securities, the Securities and Exchange Act of 1934 was enacted so that there would be federal regulation of the secondary securities market and of broker/dealers of securities. The purpose was to protect investors of marketable securities. It was believed that unregulated securities exchanges brought about the boom and depression economy that existed prior to the market crash of 1929. It was also believed that federal legislation was needed so that public companies were forced to provide full disclosure on an ongoing basis, so that investors could be informed before making securities investments.

The Securities and Exchange Act of 1934 made misrepresentation, manipulation and other abuses in the trading markets for securities illegal. The Securities and Exchange Act of 1934 established the Securities and Exchange Commission. The responsibility of the SEC is to enforce the securities laws.

The Securities and Exchange Act of 1934 required that:

- Securities listed on a stock exchange be registered
- Companies offering marketable securities make full disclosure of their financial status and changes in financial condition
- The officer and directors of corporations who control at least 10% of a company's equity securities make full disclosure of their holdings and of any transactions in the company's equity securities
- Public companies provide proxy solicitations to shareholders that allow shareholder to vote on policy matters
- Margin rules be established for securities purchased on credit
- The SEC oversees the trading practices on stock exchanges and over-the-counter markets

## Registration Requirements of New Issues of Securities

The Securities Act of 1933 was the first piece of federal legislation that regulated the sale of a company's securities (stocks and bonds). The Act required that all sales of securities must be registered with the federal government unless there was a specific exemption. The primary form of registration is the Form S-1. The purpose of the filing of this paperwork is to ensure that all material facts about the company and the securities being issued are made available to potential investors. Form S-1 contains the following information:

- A general description of the business
- An explanation of how the proceeds of the sale of securities will be used
- Historical audited financial statements
- Biographical information of each corporate officer that includes the percentage of the company's securities that each officer owns or has control over
- Any legal issues that concern the company and the securities offering
- The proposed offering price of the securities issue
- The percentage of the offering that will be paid out in underwriting commissions

## 20-Day Cooling-off Period That Occurs After the Registration of a New Securities Issue and the Filing of Form S-1

During the 20-day cooling-off period, the registration is reviewed by the Securities and Exchange Commission. If the SEC feels that there has been full and fair disclosure in the registration statement, the sale of the securities can be made after the 20-day period. If the SEC finds that there has not been full disclosure, the SEC issues a deficiency letter that requests further disclosure. The sale of securities cannot continue until the company complies with the SEC request for disclosure. The registration is not effective until the SEC declares that the disclosure made in the Form S-1 is adequate. During this 20-day period there can be no sale, solicitation, advertisement or recommendation of the securities. The only allowed activity during this time period is the distribution of a preliminary prospectus (also called a red herring) and the taking of indications of interest. Once the registration is effective, the securities issue may be sold. Solicitation of orders must be made based on the final prospectus.

### Omission or Misstatement of Material Fact in the Registration Statement

Any omission or misstatement of material fact in a registration statement or prospectus is considered fraud. The individuals affected by these omissions and misstatements and who can be prosecuted for fraud include:

- The company that issued the securities
- The lawyers that prepared the registration statement and prospectus
- The accountants that prepared the audited historical financial statements
- The underwriter that sold the securities issue

In order to avoid making omissions and misstatements of material fact, these individuals must perform a process called due diligence on the securities issue. During the due diligence process, these individuals review the registration statement and prospectus to ensure that the disclosure is adequate and truthful. The due diligence process minimizes the liability that these individuals would incur under the Securities Act of 1933.

### Liabilities That May Be Incurred by an Individual Who Signs a Registration Statement

Individuals who are signers on a registration statement may be liable for civil penalties. The civil penalties are the result of an unintentional omission or misstatement of material fact in the registration statement or prospectus. The individuals who may be affected are company directors, the accountants that prepared the financial statements, the attorneys that prepared the SEC filing and experts who prepare appraisals and reports. In order for an investor to bring a civil suit, the suit must be filed within one year of discovery of the omission or misstatement and within three years of the offering date. An investor may recover damages that equal the difference between the current market value and the price paid for the issue. When there is an intentional omission or misstatement of material fact in the registration statement or prospectus, a criminal penalty may be filed. Each offense may incur a fine of $10,000 and five years in prison.

### Securities Issues That Are Exempt from Registration Under the Securities Act of 1933

Exempt securities do not require any registration or disclosure before they can be offered for sale to the public. Most of these exempt securities include those securities offered for sale by the US government or those companies that are regulated through other laws. Securities issues that are exempt from registration include:

- Direct obligations of the US government
- Obligations of agencies that are sponsored or owned by the US government
- Municipal obligations
- Foreign government obligations
- Banker's acceptances and commercial paper that has a maturity date of less than 270 days
- Offerings of life insurance companies (such as life insurance policies and fixed annuities)
- Bank issues
- Common carrier issues (these include railroads and transportation companies)
- Issues of benevolent (or non-profit) organizations
- Issues of Small Business Investment Companies (SBICs)

## Securities Transactions That Are Exempt from Registration Under the Securities Act of 1933

Exempt transactions are those securities that are not part of a public offering, small offerings of securities, intrastate securities offerings and transactions that are not made by the issuing company. Securities transactions that are exempt from registration include:

- Securities trades that require the use of a prospectus and are exempt by Rule 144
- Intrastate offerings that are exempt by Rule 147
- Small dollar offerings that are exempt by Regulation A
- Private placements that are exempt by Regulation D
- Securities transactions that are made to non-US residents living outside the US that are exempt by Regulation S.
- Securities transactions between private individuals

## Restricted and Control Securities

Restricted securities are those securities that were purchased in unregistered and private securities offerings. Most restricted and control securities are obtained through private placements of securities, Regulation D offerings, employee stock benefit plans, as compensation for professional services or as an exchange for providing a company with start-up capital. Restricted securities are issued as a stock certificate that is stamped with a restricted legend. Restricted securities cannot be sold in a securities market unless they are registered with the SEC or are exempt from registration. Control securities are those securities that are held by an affiliate of the company that issued the securities. An affiliate is a director or shareholder that is in a position of control with the company issuing the securities. An individual has control when the individual has the ability to direct the management and policies of the company.

## Rule 144

Equity securities that are purchased in a private offering are not traded on a public securities trading market. These securities are usually purchased before a company decides to undertake an initial public offering of its stock. After the company sells a registered offering of its stock, the equity securities purchased in the private offering are not tradable on a public securities market until the restricted securities are registered with the SEC. The process for registering restricted securities with the SEC is an expensive and time-consuming process. To make this process easier, Rule 144 provides an exemption that allows small amounts of registered securities to be sold on a periodic basis without the need for registration. Rule 144 applies to the sale of restricted and control securities in the securities markets. Rule 144 allows the public resale of restricted and control securities under certain conditions.

There are five exemption requirements that must be followed in order to sell restricted or control securities:

- Restricted securities must be held for at least a year. The one-year holding period begins on the date when the securities were fully paid for. This requirement does not apply to control securities.
- The company that issued the securities must comply with the periodic reporting requirements of the SEC.

- There is a limited amount of restricted and control securities that may be sold. A maximum of 1% of the outstanding shares of the same class of securities during any three-month period may be sold. If the securities are publicly traded (listed on NYSE or NADSAQ), the average reported weekly trading volume for the four weeks preceding the filing of the notice of sale may be sold.
- The sales transaction must be executed as a routine trading transaction through a registered securities broker/dealer.
- When the sale is of more than 5,000 shares or $50,000 in any three-month period, the sale must be filed with the SEC using Form 144.

## Rule 147

Rule 147 allows a company to raise funds by selling equity securities without the need to register the securities offering with the Securities and Exchange Commission. Rule 147 only applies to intrastate offerings of equity securities. A company must meet several requirements in order to be able to take advantage of this exemption:

- The company must be incorporated in the same state in which it is selling the equity securities
- The company must conduct at least 80% of its business in the state in which it is selling the equity securities
- The company can only sell the equity securities to residents of the state in which it is selling the equity securities

The regulatory authority for intrastate offerings of equity securities is the state in which the offering is sold.

## Regulation A

Regulation A offerings are also known as Small Dollar Offerings. These offerings trade in a secondary market after the initial sale. Regulation A has two offering tiers: Tier 1 for offerings of up to $20 million in a 12-month period and Tier 2 for offerings of up to $75 million in a 12-month period. Companies that sell Regulation A offerings must file an offering statement with the SEC. The offering statement includes a notification, offering circular and exhibits. The offering circular contains the same information as a prospectus, but the financial statements do not need to be audited. Tier 2 offerings have ongoing reporting requirements; Tier 1 offerings generally do not, and Tier 1 remains subject to state ("blue sky") review, while Tier 2 offerings are not. The purpose of Regulation A offerings is to allow companies to test the waters before they go through the expense of filing an offering statement and registering the offering with the SEC. This gives companies an opportunity to determine if there is enough investor interest in their securities.

## Regulation D

Regulation D offerings are exempt from registration and prospectus requirements. Full disclosure of Regulation D offerings is made through an offering circular. Companies making a Regulation D offering should provide enough information to investors to comply with the antifraud provisions of the securities laws. There are different levels of disclosure requirements for Regulation D offerings. These levels are based on the amount of money to be raised under the securities offering.

- Rule 504 is for offerings of up to $10 million in any 12-month period. There is no requirement as to the information that must be disclosed to investors.
- Rule 506 permits offerings of an unlimited amount and is commonly relied on as Rule 506(b) [no general solicitation; allows up to 35 non-accredited but sophisticated investors, with specified disclosure obligations] or Rule 506(c) [general solicitation permitted, but sales must be limited to accredited investors with verification].

Simply stated, an accredited investor is an individual or organization that would not suffer a financial hardship if they were to lose all of the money invested in a security. An accredited investor must be one of the following:

- A financial institution, such as a bank or insurance company, which has assets that exceed $5 million
- A non-profit institutional investor, such as a charitable organization or an employee benefit plan, that has assets in excess of $5 million
- A director, executive officer, or general partner of the company selling the securities
- A business in which all the equity owners are accredited investors
- An individual with a net worth of at least $1 million
- An individual with an annual income of more than $200,000 for the past two years and a reasonable expectation of the same income level in the future
- A couple with a joint income of more than $300,000 for the past two years and a reasonable expectation of the same income level in the future
- An individual holding specified professional certifications/designations (Series 7, 82, etc.)

Non-accredited investors are sophisticated investors that understand the merits and risk of a securities investment. A non-accredited investor may or may not be able to afford the loss of the funds invested. If a non-accredited investor is not able to evaluate a securities offering, the investor will need to use the services of a purchaser representative. If a non-accredited investor is not sophisticated, the company issuing the securities offering can be sued by the non-accredited investor and the investor may be able to reclaim the full investment. To ensure that a non-accredited investor is sophisticated, the company should have the investor or the investor's purchaser representative sign an investment letter. The investment letter states that:

- The investor understands that the securities offering is not registered
- The investor understands that the securities cannot be sold in the public securities trading markets
- The investor intends to hold the securities as an investment

Regulation D applies to private placement offerings. Private placements are equity securities that are offered directly by small companies. Private placements can be sold by the company directly to investors. A broker or underwriter is not needed to facilitate the sale of the equity securities. The advantages of private placements are that they allow a company to raise needed funding quickly and the costs associated with a public offering are avoided. Private placements have the added advantage that they require less paperwork than public offerings. Private placements are limited in the amount of money that can be raised and the number of non-accredited investors that can purchase the securities. Because of this limitation, the market for the private placement securities is also limited. There is no trading market for private placements, which makes it difficult to establish a market price for private placements.

## Regulation S

Regulation S regulates the offer and sale of securities outside the US Regulation S securities are exempt from the registration requirements. If these securities are subsequently resold in the US, they must be registered prior to the sale. Regulation S permits the offshore distribution of US securities to non-US residents. Regulation S is not concerned with the citizenship of the purchaser of the securities. The purchaser may or may not be a US citizen. Regulation S is only concerned with the residency of the purchaser. In addition, a corporation or partnership that was organized under the laws of a foreign nation is considered a non-US resident and may purchase unregistered securities. Also, trusts, estates, custodians and discretionary accounts held for the benefit of non-US residents may purchase unregistered securities.

To qualify for a Regulation S exemption:

- The offer and sale must be made in an offshore transaction
- The selling efforts may not be made in the US
- The offer and sale is made to a person who does not reside in the US

## SEC Rule 134

When a new security issue is sold to the public, the offer of sale must be accompanied by a prospectus. During the 20-day cooling-off period after filing a registration statement, there is a limited amount of information that the underwriter can advertise about the new issue.

Information that can be communicated to the public without a prospectus includes:

- The name, address, phone number, email address of the issuer
- The location of the issuer's country or organization and geographic area where business is conducted
- The title, type, amount, and ranking of the securities being issued
- A description of the type of business of the issuer
- The price, yield, or interest rate of the security
- The use of proceeds of the offering
- The name, address, phone number and email address of the sender of the communication
- The name of the underwriter of the securities offering and the type of underwriting

## SEC Rule 135

When a new offering of securities is announced prior to the effective registration date, the announcement cannot be construed as being an offer to sell or an advertisement. The amount of information that a company may communicate to the public before a new issue of equity securities is limited. In all instances, the notice of the proposed registered offering is not an offer of sale.

Information that can be included in the notice includes the following:

- The name of the company offering the new issue
- The title, amount and terms of the securities offered
- The amount of the issue that includes securities being sold by security holders
- A statement of the manner and purpose of the securities offered

In no case can the company announce the name of the underwriter of the offering. The underwriter's announcement is regulated by SEC Rule 134.

## SEC Rule 137

The Securities Act prohibits the publication and distribution of research reports concerning a new issue of securities by any member of the underwriting group. SEC Rule 137 allows broker/dealers who are not a part of the underwriting group to publish and distribute research reports. A research report may be published and distributed before the registration date of a new issue of securities when:

- The broker/dealer has not participated and will not be participating in the sale of the securities
- The broker/dealer has not received any compensation or consideration from the issuer of the securities, a selling security holder, any member of the underwriting group or other individual named in the registration statement
- The broker dealer publishes and distributes the research report in the regular course of business

## SEC Rule 138

The Securities Act prohibits the making of buy-and-sell recommendations of a new issue of securities prior to the effective registration date. Under this act, members of the underwriting group are prohibited from making recommendations to buy or sell the new issue. Underwriting group members are also prohibited from making recommendations regarding securities that are convertible into a security being offered by the underwriting group.

Rule 138 allows research reports to be published and distributed when:

- The security being offered is a non-convertible security and the research report relates to the common stock of the issuer
- The security being offered is the common stock and the research report relates to the non-convertible security
- The issuer has filed all of the required reports for the preceding 12 months

## SEC Rule 139

When information about the company offering the new issue has been the subject of regularly published and distributed research reports, this information may continue during the registration period. Rule 139 allows research reports to be published and distributed during the underwriting period when:

- The publication and distribution of research reports is in the regular course of business
- Other broker/dealers are using research reports to recommend the issuer or the security offered
- The research report contains recommendations of other issuers in the same industry
- The research report lists all of the securities recommended by the broker/dealer
- All recommendations in the research report are given equal space and prominence
- The recommendation must not be more favorable than previous recommendations

## Qualified Institutional Buyer

A qualified institutional buyer is an organization that invests $100 million in securities on a discretionary basis. The issuers of these securities are not affiliated with the qualified institutional buyer. The qualified institutional buyer either trades securities for it own account or for the accounts of other qualified institutional buyers. A qualified institutional buyer may include:

- An insurance company
- An investment company or a business development company regulated by the Investment Company Act
- A Small Business Investment Company licensed by the US Small Business Administration
- An employee benefit plan
- A trust fund whose trustee is a bank or trust company

## Conditions When Unregistered Securities May Be Purchased and Sold Through Broker/Dealers

Qualified institutional buyers can trade in private placement securities. The minimum size trade for this type of transaction is $500,000. The trade must be conducted through a broker/dealer. There is a limited trading market in these large private placement securities. Institutional buyers may trade these private placement securities with other institutional buyers if the trade is executed through a broker/dealer. Rule 144A allows for the sale to be made if the following conditions are met:

- The securities are offered or sold to a qualified institutional buyer
- The buyer must provide recent publicly available financial statements
- The issuer must provide a statement of the nature of the issuer's business and its products
- The buyer understands that the securities being purchased are not of the same class of securities that the issue has listed on a securities exchange

## Obligation to Provide a Prospectus When Making an Offer to Sell a Registered Securities Issue

Transactions in securities of new issue of securities require the delivery of a prospectus at the time of the sale. Rule 174 specifies that time period in which a prospectus must be delivered for new issue securities:

- When the issuer has no other registered securities, a prospectus must be delivered for 90 days after the date of the registration statement
- When the issuer has registered shares outstanding, a prospectus must be delivered for 40 days after the date of the registration statement
- When the issuer lists the shares on a stock exchange (such as NYSE or NASDAQ), a prospectus must be delivered for 25 days after the date of the registration statement

## Manipulative or Deceptive Device

A manipulative or deceptive device includes any fraudulent act or omission to act in securities transactions. The fraud provisions of the Securities and Exchange Act apply to both exempt securities and non-exempt securities. The mail, interstate commerce and securities markets may not be used to engage in manipulative, deceptive or fraudulent behavior. Examples of manipulative behavior include:

- Creating a false or misleading appearance of active trading for a security
- Giving a false or misleading impression of the market for a security
- Circulating information that the price of a security will rise or fall because of market operations conducted to raise or lower the price of the security
- Knowingly making a false or misleading statement

- Pegging, fixing, or stabilizing the price of a security
- Employing any service, scheme or artifice to defraud
- Engaging in any act that operates as fraud or deceit

## Conflicts of Interest

The Securities and Exchange Act of 1934 addresses conflicts of interest that may arise when a research analyst makes a securities recommendation in a research report or a public appearance. Securities rules ensure that information is objective, useful and reliable. This is accomplished by:

- Restricting the approval of research reports prepared by individuals who are engaged in investment banking activities
- Restricting the approval of research reports prepared by individuals who are not directly responsible for investment research
- Limiting the supervision of research analysts to individuals who are not engaged in investment banking activities
- Protecting the publication of an unfavorable report from retaliation by those individuals engaged in investment banking activities
- Defining when underwriters of a public securities offering may and may not publish reports relating to the issuer
- Safeguarding securities analysts from review, pressure or oversight from investment banking activities

Research analysts and broker/dealers are required to disclose any conflicts of interest that are known to exist at the time of any public appearances or the distribution date of the research report. Conflicts of interest that must be disclosed include:

- The amount of debt or equity investments the research analyst or broker/dealer holds in the issuer that is the subject of the appearance or research report
- The amount of any compensation the research analyst or broker/dealer received from the issuer
- Whether or not the issuer of the securities recommended is a client of the broker/ dealer
- The amount of any compensation the research analyst received from the investment banking revenues of the broker/dealer
- Any conflicts of interest that are material to investors, research analysts or broker/dealers

## Certification Required When Making a Public Appearance

Regulation AC requires broker/dealers to record public appearances by research analysts within 30 days of the end of the calendar quarter in which the research analyst made the appearance. The research analyst must certify that:

- The views expressed by the research analyst reflect the research analyst's personal views
- No part of the compensation received by the research analyst is related to the recommendation or views of the research analyst

If certification is not obtained from the research analyst, the broker/dealer must notify the examining authority that the research analyst did not provide the certification. In addition, the broker/dealer must disclose for a 120-day period on all research reports prepared by the analyst that certification was not provided. When a research analyst is employed outside the US by a foreign company, the research analyst need only certify those public appearances made while physically in the US

## Regulation Fair Disclosure

Regulation FD was adopted to address issues related to selective disclosure and to clarify insider trading laws. The purpose of Regulation FD is to ensure the full and fair disclosure of information by issuers. Regulation FD also ensured that the prohibitions against insider trading were upheld. The issues specifically related to Regulation FD include:

- The selective disclosure of material nonpublic information by publicly traded companies and issuers
- The determination of when an insider trading liability is the result of a trader's use or knowing possession of material nonpublic information
- The incurrence of a liability because of a breach of a duty of trust or confidence in a family or non-business relationship under the misappropriation theory of insider trading

## Selective Disclosure

Selective disclosure happens when an issuer makes a distribution of material nonpublic information about a company to select individuals before making the information available to the public. These select individuals may include securities analysts or institutional investors. This practice is disruptive in that it undermines the integrity of the securities markets and decreases investor confidence in the fairness of the securities markets. In addition, selective disclosure may create a conflict of interest on the part of securities analysts. When a securities analyst receives information before it is released to the public, the securities analyst may be unwilling to make negative recommendations about an issuer, so that the securities analyst can continue to receive selectively disclosed information. Regulation FD requires that issuers disclose material information to the public using a method that reaches the public on a non-exclusive basis. This disclosure may be made either by filing the information with the SEC or through press releases.

When an issuer discloses material nonpublic information about the issuer or the securities of the issuer, that information must be made public. The public disclosure must be made simultaneously if the disclosure was intentional and promptly if the disclosure was non-intentional. This disclosure must be made when the selective disclosure was made to a person not associated with the issuer. Persons not associated with the issuer may be a broker or dealer of securities, an investment advisor, an investment company or a holder of the issuer's securities. Public disclosure is not made when the following receive material nonpublic information:

- Bankers, attorneys, accountants, or others that owe a duty of trust or confidence to the issuer
- Individuals who agree to keep the information confidential
- Organizations that issue credit ratings
- Securities brokers and others who receive the information in connection with a registered securities offering

## Records That Research Analysts Are Required to Keep and the Retention Period

The member firm with which the research analyst is associated is required to keep copies of all of the research analyst's work. This work includes, but is not limited to, all records prepared by the research analyst. Written and electronic communications, worksheets, speeches, research reports and other work performed by the research analyst must be kept on file and available for review by the appropriate regulatory authorities. These records must be retained for a period of at least three years, with the previous two year's of records kept in an easily accessible location. The location must be readily accessible in the possible occurrence of a regulatory audit.

## Regulation G

Regulation G was enacted in 2003, in response to the excesses in the securities markets, which became obvious after the market crash in 2000. These excesses occurred because start-up companies (mostly speculative issues of Internet companies) used pro-forma earnings statements. These start-up companies capitalized the money spent on building the business until the company had a regular income. These capitalized amounts did not appear on the income statement as expenses. This practice is contrary to GAAP. Under GAAP, these start-up costs would be expensed and not capitalized. This practice leads to earnings being reported at a higher amount than would be shown using GAAP. Regulation G was also enacted to limit how companies calculated cash flow.

Regulation G requires publicly traded companies to provide additional financial information when non-GAAP financial measures are released. When an issuer makes non-GAAP financial measures available, the non-GAAP financial measure must be accompanied by:

- A directly comparable financial measure that has been calculated and presented in accordance with GAAP
- A reconciliation of the differences between the non-GAAP financial measures and the most comparable financial measures calculated and presented in accordance with GAAP

In addition, non-GAAP financial measures cannot be given more prominence than GAAP financial measures. Non-GAAP financial measures must be placed and discussed separately in the issuer's financial statements. The non-GAAP information cannot appear on the face of the financial statements or in a footnote that was prepared in accordance with GAAP. In all instances, an issuer may not disclose a non-GAAP financial measure that contains an untrue statement of material fact or omits to state a material fact.

There are several situations where the dissemination of non-GAAP financial measures does not need to be accompanied by the comparable GAAP financial measures. These exemptions apply primarily to foreign private issuers. The exemptions include:

- Disclosures of non-GAAP financial measures made by a foreign private issuer when the securities will be listed on a securities exchange outside the US and the issuer is located outside the US
- Disclosures of non-GAAP financial measures that relate to a proposed business combination
- The issue is not sold to investors who are US residents

## Regulation M

Regulation M applies to secondary offerings of securities. The purpose of Regulation M is to prevent the manipulation of the price of underwritten securities prior to the effective date of the securities issue. This price manipulation occurs most often when an issuer offers additional shares of its stock for sale, when it currently has shares trading on a securities market. Regulation M applies to underwriters, market makers, issuers and selling shareholders that may have an interest in the outcome of a new securities issue. Regulation M prevents market makers in a securities issue who are also syndicate members of the securities issue to cause the price of the issue to increase prior to the effective date. Regulation M prohibits any broker or dealer who participates in the securities market for the issuer's stock to make a bid on the security or to cause another to bid for the security.

There are several activities that are exempt from Regulation M requirements. These exemptions include:

- Research activities, such as the publication and distribution of information, opinions or recommendations
- Odd-lot transactions
- The exercise of options, warrants, rights or conversion privileges
- Unsolicited brokerage transactions and unsolicited purchases that are not made through a broker, a dealer or a securities exchange
- Basket transactions of 20 or more securities in which the covered transaction does not consist of more than 5% of the value of the basket purchased
- Purchases make during the restricted period when the total is less than 2% of the average daily trading value
- Transactions in connection with a distribution
- Transactions in Rule 144A securities

## Conflict of Interest Between a Broker/Dealer and a Securities Issuer

The FINRA Conduct Rules specify that when a broker/dealer recommends a securities issue any conflict of interest between the broker/dealer and the issuer must be disclosed. The situations where a conflict of interest may exist include:

- When there is a control relationship between the broker/dealer and the issuer of the securities
- When the broker/dealer receives compensation from the securities issuer for providing advice on structuring an underwriting of a new issue of securities and the broker/dealer participates in the new issue as an underwriter
- When a broker/dealer underwrites an issue of its own securities to the public and recommends its own securities to its customers

## Control Relationship

A control relationship exists when a broker/dealer is controlled by, controls or is under common control with the issuer of a security. The control is determined by the amount of an issuer's security that the broker/dealer holds or the amount of the broker/dealer's security that an issuer holds. When a control relationship exists between a broker/dealer and the issuer of the security that is being recommended or sold by the broker/dealer, the broker/dealer must disclose the control relationship to its customers before the purchase or sale of the security. The disclosure must be made before entering into a contract with the customer. This disclosure must be made in writing and must be done before the completion of the transaction. In the normal course of business, a broker/dealer may give a verbal disclosure when making a recommendation of the security and then provide a written disclosure on the trade confirmation.

## Financial Advisory Relationship

A financial advisory relationship exists when a broker/dealer receives a fee from a customer for recommending the purchase or sale of a security. A financial advisor relationship also exists when a broker/dealer receives a fee for providing advice to a securities issuer regarding the structuring of a securities issue. When a broker/dealer provides advice to an issuer and then participates in the underwriting of the securities issue, this information must be disclosed to customers who purchase the securities in the underwriting. These underwritings may be either for primary or secondary distributions. This disclosure must be made in writing at or before the completion of the sale transaction with the customer.

## Broker/Dealer or an Affiliate of a Broker/Dealer That Is Issuing Shares of Its Own Securities

When a broker/dealer offers its debt or equity securities for sale in a public offering, the member broker/dealer and persons associated with the member are restricted from participating in the distribution. This rule also applies to issues of securities offered for sale by the parent company of the member broker/dealer and affiliates of the member broker/dealer. An affiliate is a company that controls the broker/dealer, is controlled by the broker/dealer or is under common control with the broker/dealer. In addition, when there is a conflict of interest between a company that is making a public offering and a broker/dealer or persons associated with the broker/dealer, the broker/dealer and associated persons are restricted in their participation of the distribution of the company's debt or equity securities.

## Restricting a Broker/Dealer from Selling Its Own Securities or the Securities of an Affiliate

There can be a conflict of interest when a broker/dealer sells its own debt or equity securities. This conflict of interest may arise because the broker/dealer is not considered a disinterested third party. The broker/dealer is restricted from selling its own securities and the securities of its affiliates to prevent the issue from being offered at an unfair or inflated price. This conflict of interest exists when the broker/dealer, persons associated with the broker/dealer and affiliates of the broker/dealer own 10% or more of the common equity or debt of the issuer of the securities. FINRA Rule 2720 states that the member broker/dealer may not underwrite, participate in the underwriting syndicate or selling group, or assist in the distribution of a public offering of debt or equity securities offered by the member broker/dealer or its affiliates.

## Exemptions to Rule 2720

In order for a broker/dealer to participate in the underwriting of its own securities or the securities of its affiliates, the member broker/dealer or the affiliate who is offering the securities, must have been actively engaged in the investment banking or securities business for five years prior to the filing of the registration statement. In addition, the securities issue must meet one of the following criteria:

- The price of the equity issue or the yield of a debt issue is not higher than the recommendation of a qualified independent underwriter. This underwriter must also participate in the preparation of the registration statement, prospectus and offering circular.
- A bona fide independent market exists for the class of securities as of the date of the filing of the registration statement and the effective date of the offering.
- The class of securities is rated Baa or higher by Moody's rating service or is rated Bbb or higher by Standard & Poor's rating service.

## Disclosure Required by a Broker/Dealer Selling Its Own Securities or the Securities of Its Affiliates

When a member broker/dealer offers its securities to the public, the member broker/dealer must disclose the date the offering is expected to be completed and how the proceeds of the offering will be released from the escrow account. This disclosure must be made in the registration statement, offering circular or a similar document. The registration statement or offering circular must disclose that the offering is being made under the provisions of Rule 2720. The registration statement or offering circular must also state that the offering is being made by the broker/dealer or affiliate, the name of the qualified independent underwriter and that the underwriter assumes the responsibility for pricing the offering and for performing due diligence.

### Types of Investors Who May Purchase the Securities Issued by a Broker/Dealer or Its Affiliates

When a broker/dealer recommends that a customer purchase the securities of the broker/dealer or of an affiliate of the broker/dealer, the broker/dealer must ensure that the investment is suitable for the customer. This suitability is based on information supplied by the customer that applies to the customer's investment objectives, financial situation and financial needs. This information must be maintained in the records of the broker/dealer. These records must be maintained by the broker/dealer for three years. When the purchase of an issue of securities is for a discretionary account, the owner of the discretionary account must give the broker/dealer written approval for the purchase.

### New Issue

A new issue is an initial public offering of an equity security made in accordance with Section 3(a)(11) of the Securities Exchange Act of 1934. A new issue is filed with the Securities and Exchange Commission in the form of a registration statement and offered for sale to the public with an offering circular. A new issue is not a secondary issue of a currently issued or traded security. For the purpose of Rule 2790, a new issue does not include certain private offerings, offerings of exempted securities, securities of a commodity pool, rights offerings, exchange offerings, offerings of investment grade asset-backed securities, offerings of convertible and preferred securities, securities of an investment company and securities that have a market outside the United States.

### Restricted Person

A restricted person is any person or entity that meets one of the following criteria:

- A broker/dealer who is a member of FINRA or any other broker/dealer
- Personnel of a broker-dealer. Personnel include officers, directors, general partners, associated persons or employees of a broker/dealer. Also included are immediate family members of broker/dealer personnel.
- Finders and fiduciaries of the managing underwriter such as attorneys, accountants and financial consultants.
- Portfolio managers that have the authority to buy and sell securities for a bank, savings and loan, insurance company, investment company, investment advisor or investment account. Also included are immediate family members of portfolio managers.
- A person who owns 10% or more of a broker/dealer.

### FINRA Rule 5130

Rule 5130 covers restrictions on the purchase and sale of initial equity public offerings. The goal of Rule 5130 is to ensure that member broker/dealers make bona fide public offerings of securities at the offering price, that broker/dealers do not withhold these securities from the public for the benefit of the broker/dealer and that insiders associated with the security being sold do not use their insider knowledge at the expense of public customers who wish to purchase the security in the initial public offering. The purpose of Rule 5130 is to maintain investor confidence in the securities markets and to ensure that initial public offerings remain a viable option for companies wishing to raise capital for their future growth and expansion.

Rule 5130 prohibits the following purchases and sales of initial public offerings:

- Any FINRA member or any person associated with a member is prohibited from buying or selling a new issue for accounts owned by a restricted person or accounts in which a restricted person has a beneficial interest.

- The rule prohibits member broker/dealers from holding any issues that were acquired by the member broker/dealer when acting as an underwriter or selling group member.
- The sale or purchase of shares of an initial public offering between members of the selling group may not be transferred or sold to a non-restricted person at the public offering price.
- A broker/dealer may not sell or purchase a new issue at the public offering price as part of an accommodation to a non-restricted person.
- A broker/dealer that is organized as an investment partnership may only purchase a new issue at the public offering price as long as the purchase is credited to the capital accounts of its partners.

Member broker/dealers are required to pre-qualify any account to which the broker/dealer intends to sell shares of a new issue. The information must have been obtained within the twelve months prior to the sale. The broker/dealer must obtain a representation from beneficial owners that state that the account is eligible to purchase shares of a new issue. The representation from the beneficial owner may be obtained from the account holder or a person authorized to represent the beneficial owner. Conduits such as banks, foreign banks, broker/dealers or investment advisors must certify that the purchase of the new issue is in compliance with Rule 5130. The information collected from beneficial owners and conduits must be in writing. A copy of the information that relates to the eligibility of the account to purchase a new issue must be maintained by the broker/dealer for three years following the last sale of a new issue to that account.

Rule 5130 does not apply to sales and purchases to investors that meet the following criteria:

- Investment companies registered under the Investment Company Act of 1940
- Common trust funds that have investments from 1000 or more accounts and that are not limited to trust accounts of restricted persons
- Separate or investment accounts of insurance companies that are funded by premiums from 1000 or more policyholders and are not limited principally to restricted persons
- Accounts that do not exceed 10% of the beneficial interests of restricted persons
- Publicly traded companies that are either listed on a national securities exchange, traded on the Nasdaq Global Market or are a foreign issuer
- Investment companies organized under the laws of a foreign jurisdiction
- Employee Retirement Income Security Act benefits plans

In some initial public offerings, the issuer of the securities may specify that a certain amount of the new issue will be distributed to specified individuals. In most cases, these new issue securities will be set aside for the issuer's officers, employees and key suppliers. An issuer may also specify that shares of the new issue securities are to be distributed to a broker/dealer, the broker/dealer's employees or the broker/dealer's fiduciaries and finders. This is only allowed if these individuals and employees are also employees or directors of the issuer. The intent of Rule 5130 is that new issues of securities are mainly sold to the public and not to industry insiders. An underwriter may only purchase shares of a new issue if the issue is undersubscribed. A new issue is undersubscribed when there is a low demand for the issue. The underwriter may only place these shares in its investment account and not into the accounts of restricted persons.

## FINRA RULE 2241

Rule 2241 places the following restrictions on the control the investment banking department can have over the research department:

- Investment banking cannot supervise or control a research analyst.
- Investment banking cannot influence a research analyst's compensation evaluation.
- Investment banking cannot review a research report before publication.

Investment banking may only review a research report before publication in order to ensure the accuracy of the information or to identify potential conflicts of interest. This may occur under the following conditions:

- Written communication with the research analyst is made through legal or compliance personnel.
- Oral communication is documented and made in the presence of legal or compliance personnel.

Rule 2241 places the following restrictions on communications between issuers and research analysts:

- A research report cannot be submitted to the subject company before publication of the research report.
- The subject company may only review the research report before publication in order to verify the factual accuracy of information.
- A research analyst cannot participate in the solicitation of investment banking business. This includes participating in road shows, communicating with current and prospective customers and engaging in sales and marketing efforts.
- Communication between a research analyst and a customer that concerns investment banking must be fair, balance and not misleading.

Rule 2241 places the following restrictions on research analyst compensation:

- Research analysts cannot receive any bonus, salary or other compensation based on a specific investment banking service.
- A committee must review and approve the compensation paid to a research analyst. This review must be performed annually and reported to the member's board of directors.
- Investment banking may not be represented on the compensation review committee.
- The committee must consider the research analyst's performance, the correlation between recommendations and investment performance and recommendations from the member's clients and employees.
- The compensation review cannot take into account the research analyst's contribution to the investment banking business.
- The basis for the research analyst's compensation must be documented.
- The committee must make an annual attestation of the review.

Rule 2241 places the following restriction on research analysts when publishing research reports and making public appearances on behalf of a subject company:

- An underwriter of a new issue cannot publish a research report or make a public appearance for 40 days after the offering date.
- An underwriter of offering is prohibited from publishing a research report or making a public appearance for 10 days after the offering date.
- An underwriting group member cannot publish a research report or make a public appearance for 25 days after the offering date.
- A party to a lock-up agreement is prohibited from publishing a research report or making a public appearance for the 15 days prior to and after the expiration, waiver or termination of the lock-up agreement.
- Notice must be given before research coverage of a subject company is terminated. A final research report must be published that is comparable in scope to previous research reports and that contains a final recommendation.

Rule 2241 governs how a member broker/dealer rates securities of an issuer and sets price targets for an issue. It does not oversee the ratings or rating system used by a member. It does require that:

- The meaning of each rating used in the rating system is clearly defined.
- The rating given to an issue must be consistent with the definition of the rating.

The following information must be disclosed in all published research reports that contain a rating:

- The percentage of securities given a buy, hold/neutral, or sell rating.
- The percentage of subject companies with a buy, hold/neutral, or sell rating for which the member provided investment banking services in the past 12 months.
- That the information is current at the end of the last calendar quarter.

## Rule 2210

Rule 2210 governs communications with the public by a member firm. These communications include performance advertising. Rule 2210 states that all member communications with the public must be based on principles of fair dealing and good faith. These communications should provide an investor with enough information to provide a sound basis for evaluating the facts in regard to a security, a type of security, an industry or a service. The rule also states that members may not omit any material fact or qualification if the omission would cause the communication to be misleading. Rule 2210 also states that any violation by a member of an SEC rule applicable to member communications with the public will be deemed a violation of Rule 2210.

Rule 2210 defines the six types of communications as follows:

- Advertisement is material that is published in print, public and electronic media. It includes the Internet, television, newspaper, magazine and radio. It does not include reprints and institutional sales material.
- Sales literature that is written and electronic communications distributed to the public. It includes research reports, market letters, and performance reports.
- Correspondence to existing and prospective customers includes all mail messages a member sends to one or more existing customers and less than 25 prospective customers within a 30 day period.

- Institutional sales material includes communications that are only distributed to institutional investors.
- A public appearance is any participation in a seminar, forum, interview or public speaking activity.
- Independently prepared reprint is an excerpt out of a publication. The excerpt may be an entire article or portions of an article.

## Approval Requirements for Communications with the Public

A registered principal of the member firm must approve all advertisements, sales literature and independently prepared reprints. The following requirements must be met:

- The principal must sign or initial and date these communications before being distributed or filed with FINRA Advertising Regulation Department.
- A supervisory analyst may sign or initial research reports.
- Sales literature concerning security futures may be signed or initialed by a registered principal qualified to supervise security futures activities.
- Communication that has been approved by the FINRA Advertising Regulation Department is exempt from the approval requirements.

## Recordkeeping Requirements for Communications with the Public

A member firm must maintain all advertisements, sales literature and independently prepared reprints. These must be kept in a separate file and maintained for three years from the date of last issue. The file must include:

- A copy of the advertisement, sales literature or independently prepared reprint. The dates of first and last use of the communication must be noted.
- The name of the registered principal who approved each communication and the date of the approval.
- For exempt communication, the name of the member that filed the communication with the FINRA Advertising Regulation Department. The review letter from the department should be included.
- The sources for statistical tables, charts, graphs and other illustrations used in communications with the public must also be maintained.

## Filing Requirements When Submitting Correspondence for Review to the FINRA Advertising Regulation Department

The following are required when a member files advertisements and sales literature for review:

- The actual or proposed date of first use, the name of the registered principal who approved the communication and the date of the approval.
- Communications regarding registered investment companies, public direct participation programs, government securities or investment analysis tools must be filed within 10 days of first use or publication.
- Bond mutual fund related communications that include mutual fund volatility ratings must be filed 10 days prior to use.
- Communications regarding registered investment companies, collateralized mortgage obligations and security futures must be filed 10 days prior to use.

### Disclosure Requirements for Bond Mutual Fund Volatility Ratings

The following disclosures must accompany any supplemental sales literature that includes a bond mutual fund volatility rating:

- That the disclosure statement complies with Rule 2210 and any additional information that would help an investor understand the rating.
- All of the current bond mutual fund volatility ratings that have been issued for the fund.
- The name of the entity that issued the rating.
- The current rating, the date of the rating and the reason for any change in the current rating from the prior rating.
- A narrative of the description of the rating, the criteria and method used to determine the rating, whether consideration was paid for the rating, the risks measured by the rating and that the fund is not guaranteed to hold the same rating in the future.

### Standards and Reporting Requirements for Security Futures Communications with the Public

All communications with the public regarding security futures should follow these standards:

- A discussion of the risks involved in investing in security futures
- A statement that security futures are not suitable for all investors
- A statement that documentation for claims, comparisons, recommendations and statistics will be supplied upon request
- The information must not be misleading or inconsistent

A file of advertisements and sales literature regarding security futures must be maintained for a period of three years. The file must contain the names of the people who prepared and approved the communication. It should also name the source of any recommendation.

### Disclosure Requirements in Communications with the Public Regarding Security Futures

Certain types of communications regarding security futures are exempt from providing a security futures risk disclosure statement. These communications may contain:

- A description of security futures
- A list of registered clearing agencies for security futures
- A description of the security exchange where the security future is traded
- A discussion of how the security future is priced

Communications with the public regarding security futures are exempt from disclosure if:

- The communication only provides a general description of the security future.
- The communication lists the contact information where the security futures risk disclosure statement can be obtained.
- The communication does not contain recommendations or performance figures.

Projections may be included in security futures sales literature and correspondence under the following conditions:

- Must be accompanied or preceded by the security futures risk disclosure statement
- There is no guarantee of future performance

- Performance figure parameters are established
- Commissions, fees and interest charges are disclosed
- Projections are used as a source of reference or to develop a recommendation
- Material assumptions are clearly identified
- Risks are disclosed

## Collateralized Mortgage Obligation (CMO)

A collateralized mortgage obligation is a multi-class debt security backed by pass-through securities or mortgage loans. The education material that must be provided to a customer before a sale transaction is executed includes:

- A discussion of the characteristics and risks; for example, credit quality, prepayment rates, interest rates, tax considerations, costs and liquidity
- A discussion of the structure of the CMO
- A discussion of the relationship between mortgage loans and mortgage securities
- Answers to potential questions
- A glossary of terms

All communications with the public regarding CMO's must contain:

- The name of the product and the term "collateralized mortgage obligation"
- No comparisons with other investments
- If applicable, that government agency backing applies only to the face value and not to premiums paid
- A disclosure that the yield and average life fluctuates based on the rate at which mortgage holders prepay the underlying mortgages and the current interest rate

## Institutional Sales Material and Institutional Investor

Institutional sales material is any communication that is provided solely to institutional investors. A member may not distribute institutional sales material if the member has reason to believe the information will be forwarded to a person other than an institutional investor. Institutional sales material must be approved by a registered principal of institutional sales material and maintained for three years. An institutional investor may be any one of the following:

- A bank, savings and loan, insurance company or registered investment company
- A registered investment advisor
- Any entity with at least $50 million in total assets
- A government entity
- An employee benefit plan
- A FINRA member
- A person acting on behalf of an institutional investor

## Options Communications

All options communications must be approved by the member firm and by the FINRA regulatory process. The compliance registered options principal of the member must approve all advertisements, educational material and sales literature prior to distribution to the public. The member must maintain a record of the names of the people who prepared the options communication, the name of the person that gave the approval and the source of any recommendations. This information must be kept in an easily accessible place for three years. In addition, the communication must be submitted to the FINRA Advertising/Investment Companies

Regulation Department 10 days prior to use. The communication cannot be used until approved by the regulation department. There is also a spot-check procedure to which a member firm may be subjected. FINRA makes routine written requests to members and requests the submission of options advertising and sales literature material.

Rule 2220 defines three types of options communications with the public:

- Advertisements are directed at a mass audience using a public media such as newspaper, magazine, radio, television, film, video and billboard. Advertisements are not required to be accompanied or preceded by an option disclosure statement.
- Educational material is provided to customers or the public. The purpose of educational material is to explain the nature of standardized options markets or options strategies.
- Sales literature is a written communication distributed to customers or the public. Sales literature contains analysis, performance reports, projections or recommendations regarding options. Information communicated during seminars and lectures that pertains to options is also considered sales literature.

All advertisements, educational material, sales literature and other communications used by a member firm which concern options must meet the following standards:

- The communication may not contain any untrue statements or omissions of material fact that may be false or mislead the public.
- The communication may not contain an indication of specific results, exaggerated statements or unwarranted claims.
- Opinions and forecasts must have a sound basis, be clearly labeled and be warranted.
- The communication cannot constitute a prospectus as defined in the Securities Act of 1933.

When an options communication discusses the uses or advantages of options, the risks involved in options transactions and the complexities of options investment strategies must be addressed in all advertisements, educational materials and sales literature. These communications should also inform investors that options are not a suitable investment for all investors. When preparing options communications, the following guidelines should be observed:

- Statements regarding the potential opportunities and advantages of options must include a statement of the risks involved.
- The communication should state that options are not suitable for all investors.
- The communication cannot include statements that suggest a secondary market for options will not be made.

### *Advertisements*

Advertisements are exempt from disclosure if the material complies with SEC Rule 134. In order to comply, the advertisement must:

- Limit information to a general description of the securities being offered and of the issuer
- State the name and address where an options disclosure document may be obtained
- Not include recommendations, performance figures or annualized rates of return

Examples of exempt advertising include:

- The advertisement contains a brief description of the option, the attributes and operation of the options exchange and how the option is priced.
- The advertisement includes a statement required by a state law or administrative authority.
- The designs, logos, typefaces, headlines and photographs used in the advertisement are not misleading.

### *Educational Materials That Are Exempt from Disclosure*

Educational materials are exempt from disclosure if the material complies with SEC Rule 134A. In order to comply, the educational material must meet the following guidelines:

- The risks involved in options trading and the strategies addressed in the material must be explained.
- Performance figures and annualized rates of returns cannot be used in the material.
- There is no recommendation to purchase or sell an option contract.
- The only securities identified are those that are exempt from registration, index options and foreign currency options.
- The name and address where an options disclosure document can be obtained must be listed in the material.

### *Options Sales Literature*

Sales literature that discusses any aspect of options must conform to the following guidelines:

- The supporting documentation for any claims made in the sales literature should be made available upon request and so stated in the sales literature.
- Projected performance figures are allowed if no guarantee of future performance is indicated.
- The performance figure parameters are clearly established.
- Commissions, interest charges and other costs must be disclosed.
- Projections are used only as a source of reference or as a comparative device.
- All material assumptions are clearly identified.
- The risks involved in options transactions are discussed.

Records and statistics which show the past performance of recommendations or transactions may be used in options sales literature if the following apply:

- The records and statistics are described in a balanced manner and cover at least the past 12-month period.
- The communication includes the date and price of each recommendation or transaction.
- Commissions, interest charges and annualized rates of return are disclosed.
- The communication describes the market conditions during the period covered.
- A statement that the results presented are not an indication of future performance
- A Registered Options Principal must determine that the records and statistics are representative of the recommendation.

## Rule 472

### *Advertising*

An advertisement is any communication that is published or used in print, electronic or other public media. This public media includes newspapers, periodicals, magazines, radio, television, telephone recordings, web sites, motion pictures, audio and video devices, telecommunications devices, billboards and signs. All advertisements must be approved prior to use by an allied member, supervisory analyst or other person described in Rule 342(b)(1), as long as this person is not the preparer of the advertisement. An advertisement that is for a public offering of a security must comply with the registration requirement of the Securities Act of 1933. The name of the member firm must appear in all advertisements, excluding recruitment advertisements.

### Market Letter

A market letter is a written comment on the condition of the market. Market letters may also recommend specific securities as long as they comply with the standards of Rule 472(j). The amount of information contained in a market letter is limited and supporting information must be offered. Market letters may include follow-ups to research reports and articles written by the member firm that are published in magazines. Market letters are generally limited to one page. Market letters must be approved in advance of their distribution. This approval may be given by an allied member, supervisory analyst or person designated under Rule 342(b)(1). The person who prepared the market letter may not give the approval.

### Sales Literature

Sales literature is any written or electronic material that discusses or promotes the products, services and facilities offered by the member firm or its personnel. Sales literature may also be a telemarketing script. Sales literature may include a discussion of how an investment may fit into an individual's financial plan. Sales literature may also include references to market letters, research reports, brochures or other communications published by the member firm. This approval may be given by an allied member, supervisory analyst or person designated under Rule 342(b)(1). The person who prepared the sales literature may not give the approval.

### Public Appearance

A public appearance is any participation by a member firm, its allied members or employees in a seminar, public forum, interactive electronic forum, radio or television interview or other public speaking appearance where the research analyst makes a recommendation or offers an opinion on an equity security. These public appearances must be approved in advance of publication or broadcast. This approval may be given by an allied member, supervisory analyst or person designated under Rule 342(b)(1). In addition, the member firm must set written supervisory procedures for allied members and employees who make public appearances.

### Research Report

A research report is a written or electronic communication that includes an analysis of equity securities, individual companies or industries. The information included in the research report should be complete and sufficient enough to base an investment decision. If there is a question as to whether a document is a research report or a market letter, the document should be treated as a research report. Research reports must be approved by a qualified supervisory analyst. If the supervisory analyst does not have the technical expertise in a particular product area, the analysis contained in the research report may be co-approved by a product specialist of the member firm.

### *General Standards for All Communications with the Public*

Rule 472 sets general standards that apply to all communications with the public published by a member firm. Rule 472 states that a member firm may not publish any communication which contains:

- An untrue statement or omission of a material fact that is false or misleading.
- The promise of a specific result or return.
- An exaggerated or unwarranted claim.
- An opinion that does not have a reasonable basis.
- A projection or forecast that is not clearly labeled as a forecast.

Rule 472 also sets specific standards that apply to recommendations, records of past performance, projections and predictions, comparisons, dating reports, identification of sources and testimonials.

### *Recommendations, Projections and Predictions, Comparisons and Dating Reports*

When a recommendation is used in a communication, it must follow these guidelines:

- The basis of the recommendation must be substantiated as reasonable.
- Supporting information must be provided or offered.
- The market price of the security at the time the recommendation is made must be indicated.
- When projections and predictions are used in a communication, the basis or assumption for the projection must be included and the materials used must be made available upon request.
- Comparisons of a member firm's service, personnel, facilities or charges must be supported by facts.
- All communications should be appropriately dated and information that is not current must be identified.

### *Records of Past Performance*

Rule 472 requires that the following conditions be met in communications that include records or statistics regarding the performance of past recommendations or of actual transactions:

- The records of past performance must be balanced, specific to the recommendation or transaction and cover the previous 12-month period.
- The date and price of each initial recommendation or transaction must be included.
- The date and price of the recommendation or transaction at the end of the period or at liquidation must be included.
- Costs, commissions, interest charges and other applicable expenses must be disclosed.
- An indication of the general market conditions during the period covered must be included.
- A statement must be made that the results presented are not an indicator of future performance.
- A record of recommendations and evidence of actual transaction on which the record is based must be maintained by the member firm for 3 years.

### Use of Sources and Testimonials in Communications with the Public

When a member firm publishes a communication that includes information from an external source, the following guidelines apply:

- When the member firm does not have direct supervision over the communication, the name of the individual or outside organization that prepared the material must be included.
- When the member firm has direct supervision of a correspondent member firm that prepared the communication, the member firm must disclose this information when the material is distributed.
- When the issuer prepares a communication that is distributed by a member firm, the preparer and publisher must be identified in the material.

Testimonials about the quality of a member firm's investment advice must include:

- A statement that the testimonial may not represent the experience of other clients.
- If a fee was paid for the testimonial.
- If the testimonial concerns a technical aspect of investing, the person making the testimonial must have the knowledge and experience to make a valid opinion.

### Disclosures That Are Required

The front page of a research report must include the disclosures required by Rule 472. These disclosures must be clear, comprehensive and prominent. The following must be disclosed in research reports:

- If the member firm or its affiliates managed or co-managed a public offering for, or received compensation for, investment banking services from a subject company in the past 12 months.
- If the member firm makes a market in the subject company's securities.
- If the member firm or its affiliates own 1% or more of the common equity securities of the subject company on the last day of the month preceding the publication of the research report.
- Price targets, the valuation methods used and price objectives must have a reasonable basis and include a discussion of risks.
- The meanings of all the ratings used in the rating system must be provided. Definitions of ratings must be consistent with their meaning.

### Compensation Disclosures That Are Required and Must Be Made by Member Firms

Member firms must include the following disclosures in published research reports:

- Compensation received by research analysts from the subject company during the past 12 months.
- Compensation received by research analysts that is based on the member firm's investment banking revenues.
- If the subject company has been a client of the member firm during the 12 months prior to the publication of the research report.
- Investment banking services, non-investment banking-securities related services and non-securities services provided to the subject company.
- Compensation received by the member firm for products or services other than investment banking services from the subject company during the past 12 months.

### *Other Disclosures That Are Required and Must Be Made by Research Analysts and Member Firms*

Research analysts and member firms must include the following disclosures in published research reports:

- Compensation received by an affiliate of the member firm for products or services other than investment banking services from the subject company during the past 12 months
- If the research analyst or a household member has a financial interest in the securities of the subject company and the nature of the financial interest
- If the research analyst or a household member is an officer, director, or board member of the subject company
- If there is any conflict of interest that is known to the research analyst
- For research reports that cover 6 or more subject companies, the required disclosures may be provided using a hyperlink, a web site address, a toll free number or a postal address

### *Disclosures That Apply When a Research Analyst Makes a Public Appearance*

When a research analyst makes a public appearance, the research analyst and the member firm must disclose any ownership of securities, compensation and other relationships with the subject company. Rule 472 specifically states that the following must be disclosed in a public appearance:

- If the member firm or its affiliates own 1% or more of the common equity securities of the subject company
- If the research analyst or a household member has a financial interest in the securities of the subject company and the nature of the financial interest
- If the subject company is a client of the member firm during the 12 months prior to the public appearance
- If the member firm or it affiliates received any compensation from the subject company
- Any material conflict of interest of the research analyst or the member firm
- If the research analyst or a household member is an officer, director or board member of the subject company
- If the research analyst received compensation from the subject company in the 12 months prior to the public appearance

### *Disclosure Exemptions*

Rule 472 allows for the following exemptions to the information that must be disclosed in research reports:

- When a third party research report is distributed, the member firm must provide a web address where the applicable disclosures may be found.
- The disclosure requirements do not apply to third party research reports that the member firm makes available to its customers.
- A supervisory analyst must approve third party research reports distributed by the member firm.
- The third party research report does not contain any input from the member firm or its affiliates.

### *Approval Process for Communications with the Public and Research Reports*

Advertisements, market letters, sales literature and other types of communications that are distributed to the public by a member firm must be approved by an allied member, a supervisory analyst or other qualified person as described in Rule 342(b)(1). This person must be a Series 14 compliance officer. Research reports must be approved in advance by a supervisory analyst as described in Rule 344. This approval must occur before the first use of the communication. This approval cannot be given by a Series 9 or Series 10 Branch Manager. The Series 9 and Series 10 branch managers can only approve written communications of an individual nature to a customer that are created at the branch office level. Rule 472 applies to form letters, advertisements, sales literature, market letters and research reports that are written or electronically transmitted. Also included in this approval requirement are lectures, seminars, TV and radio appearances and magazine articles.

### *When a Communication That Has Been Prepared by an External Source Is Exempt from Approval*

Communications with the public that have been prepared by an external source are exempt from approval when the following conditions are met:

- The member firm does not have editorial control over the content, subject matter or timing of the communication
- The material is available to other member firms and was not prepared at the request of the member firm
- The preparer of the material is subject to a comparable system of regulation as the member firm.
- The material is transmitted in its entirety and does not contain any comments by the member firm.

### *Relationship Between the Research and Investment Banking Departments of a Member Firm*

To avoid the possibility of a conflict of interest, there are limitations on the interactions between the investment banking and research departments of a member firm. Rule 472 states that:

- Research analysts may not be subject to the supervision or control of a member's investment banking department.
- The investment banking department may not have any influence or control over the compensatory evaluation of a research analyst.
- The investment banking department and employees who are not directly responsible for investment research may not review or approve research reports before publication of the research report.
- Research reports may be reviewed by employees who are not a part of the research department to verify the factual accuracy of information or to identify potential conflicts of interest. The review must be made through the member's legal or compliance departments.

### *Relationship Between the Research Department of a Member Firm and the Subject of the Research Report*

The limitations on the interactions between the research department of a member firm and the company that is the subject of a research report include:

- A member firm may not submit a research report to the subject company prior to publication, except to review sections to verify facts.
- A member firm may not provide the subject company with the research summary, the research rating or the price target contained in the report.
- The legal or compliance department of the member firm must be provided with a complete draft of the report before it is submitted to the subject company.

- If the research department changes the rating or price target after submitting the research report to the subject company, the changes must be authorized by the legal or compliance department.
- The member firm may not notify the subject company that a rating will be changed until after the close of trading one business day prior to the announcement of the change.
- Research analysts are prohibited from engaging in investment banking activities.

### *Investment Banking Activities in Which Research Analysts and Investment Banking Personnel May Not Participate*

Research analysts are prohibited from directly or indirectly:

- Participating in a road show related to an investment banking services transaction
- Communicating with a current or prospective customer about an investment banking services transaction

Investment banking personnel are prohibited from directly or indirectly:

- Directing a research analyst to participate in any sales or marketing efforts related to an investment banking services transaction
- Directing a research analyst to communicate with a current or prospective customer about an investment banking services transaction

Written or oral communications delivered by research analysts to current or prospective customers that discuss investment banking services transactions must be fair, balanced and not misleading.

### *Restrictions Placed on the Trading of Securities*

Research analysts and their household members are restricted from trading securities under the following conditions:

- Research analysts and their household members may not purchase an issuer's securities prior to its initial public offering if the issuer is in the same type of business as companies that the research analyst covers in research reports.
- Research analysts and their household members may not trade in a subject company's securities for 30 calendar days prior to and 5 calendar days after the publication of a research report containing information about the subject company or a change in the rating or price target.
- Research analysts and their household members may not make a trade that is inconsistent with the research analyst's current recommendation.

### *Situations Allowed Where a Research Analyst May Trade the Securities of a Subject Company*

Research analysts and their household members may purchase or sell the securities of a subject company under the following conditions:

- The transaction has been pre-approved in writing by the legal or compliance department of the member firm and the transaction is due to an unanticipated significant change in the research analyst's financial condition.
- The sale transaction is made within the first 30 calendar days of the research analyst's employment with the member firm.

- The sale transaction is made within 30 calendar days from the date of the publication of the research report as long as the research analyst had purchased the subject company's securities prior to any coverage in a research report.
- If the research analyst or household member does not have control of the investment account.
- The transaction is in a registered diversified investment company.

### *Limitations on Publishing Research Reports by Member Firms That Participate in the Securities Offerings of a Subject Company*

When a member firm participates in a securities offering of a company that is the subject of a research report, the following restrictions apply:

- If the member firm acts as underwriter or dealer of an initial public offering, a research report regarding the issuer and opinions regarding the security may not be made within 10 calendar days following the offering date.
- If the member firm acts as manager or co-manager of a secondary offering, a research report regarding the issuer and opinions regarding the security may not be made within 3 calendar days following the offering date.

### *Limitations Placed on Compensation*

Rule 472 places restrictions on the compensation paid to research analysts. These restrictions state that:

- Research analysts may not receive any compensation incentive or bonus for specific investment banking services transactions. Research analysts may receive compensation based on the member firm's overall performance.
- A committee must review the compensation paid to research analysts on an annual basis. This committee reports to the board of directors or to a senior executive officer of the member firm. This committee may not include representatives of the investment banking department.

The committee must consider the following factors in the review:

- The research analyst's individual performance
- The correlation between recommendations and stock price performance
- The ratings received from clients, peers and independent rating services
- The research analyst's contribution to the investment banking business of the member firm may not be considered in the review

## Rule 791

### *General Guidelines That Apply to Communications with Customers That Concern Options*

According to Rule 791, member firms, allied members and employees of member firms shall not distribute any advertisement, educational material, sales literature or other communication to a customer or the public that contains the following:

- An untrue statement or omission of material fact that is false or misleading.
- A promise of specific results, unwarranted claims, opinions that do not have a reasonable basis or forecasts of future events that are unwarranted.

- A hedge clause or disclaimer which is not legible, which disclaims responsibility for the content of the communication or is inconsistent with the communication
- Would constitute a prospectus as defined under the Securities Act of 1933

### Advertisement, Educational Material and Sales Literature

Advertisement, educational material and sales literature are defined as:

- An advertisement is a sales communication that broadcasts to the public using newspapers, periodicals, magazines, radio, television, telephone, film, billboards and signs.
- Educational material includes advertisements and explanatory material that is made available to the public. This material may contain explanations of how options markets work and descriptions of various options strategies.
- Sales literature is written communication that is distributed to customers or the public that contains an analysis, performance report, projection or recommendations or market conditions. This information is usually made available at seminars, lectures and similar public appearances.

### Standards to Which Advertisements Must Conform

Advertisements that contain a discussion of options must meet the following standards:

- Advertisements that describe or refer to any option must be accompanied by an Options Disclosure Document or the document must be made available. The advertisement should include the name and address of the person from whom the document may be obtained.
- Advertisements may only contain a general description of the security or of the issuer.
- Advertisements may include a short description of the option, the general attributes of the option, the operation of the markets and how option prices are determined.
- Advertisements may include statements required by state law or administrative authority.
- Advertisements may not be misleading.
- Advertisements may not include recommendations, performance figures or annualized rates of return.

### Disclosures of Risk to Be Included in Communications with the Public

All advertisements, educational material or sales literature that discusses the uses or advantages of options shall include:

- A statement of the risks involved in options transactions and options investment strategies
- A statement that options are not suitable for all investors
- A statement regarding the potential opportunities or advantages of options investing must be balanced with a statement of the corresponding risks
- Statements that suggest the availability of a secondary market for options are prohibited

### Standards to Which Sales Literature Must Conform

Sales literature that contains a discussion of options must meet the following standards:

- Claims, comparisons, recommendations, statistics and other information will be supplied upon request
- Projected performance figures may be included as long as no indication of future performance is made, performance figure parameters are clearly established, relevant costs are disclosed, projections are reasonable, projections are used as a source of reference or comparative device, material assumptions are clearly identified and risks are discussed.

- Records and statistics of past recommendations may be used if the portrayal is balanced and based on the past 12 month period, the date and price of each recommendation must be stated, all relevant costs are disclosed and there is an indication of general market conditions.
- There must be a statement that the results presented are not an indication of future performance.
- A registered options principal determines that the records or statistics represent the recommendation or transaction reported upon.

### *Approval Required for Options Communications*

Options communications must be approved by both a compliance registered options principal of the member firm and by the New York Stock Exchange.

- All options related advertisements, educational material and sales literature must be approved prior to publication by a compliance registered options principal.
- The communication must be retained by the member firm for three years. The material must include the name of the person who prepared the material, the name of the person that approved the material and the sources of any recommendations. The material must be kept in an easily accessible place and available for examination by the Exchange.
- All options related advertisements and educational materials must be submitted to the Exchange 10 days prior to first use. The material may not be used until it is approved by the Exchange.
- Options advertisements and educational materials that have been approved by a comparable regulatory agency are exempt from Exchange approval.
- Advertisements that reference options in a listing of services are exempt from Exchange approval.
- The material must be accompanied by an Options Disclosure Document.

## Rule 2110

Rule 2110 discusses a member firm's ability to trade in a security prior to the publication of a research report that covers that security. This limitation is placed on member firms so that firms may not adjust or establish an inventory position in the security prior to the publication of a research report. Rule 2110 prohibits a firm from accumulating a position in a security to meet customer demand for the security after the publication of a favorable research report. Rule 2110 attempts to ensure just and equitable principles of trade, by preventing member firms from filling customer orders from the member firm's inventory.

### *Trading Activities That Are Prohibited*

The following trading activities are regulated by Rule 2110:

- Any trading activity that establishes, increases, decreases or liquidates a member firm's position in a security prior to the publication of a research report does not conform with just and equitable principles of trade.
- Any change in a member firm's inventory position that is intended to alter the firm's position in anticipation of investor interest after publication of the research report is prohibited.
- Member firm's may develop and implement policies and procedures that prohibit the trading department from gaining advance knowledge of the information contained in a research report.

## Rule 2711 (now FINRA 2241)

Rule 2711 is the response to Section 15D of the Securities Exchange act of 1934. Rule 2711 governs the research departments of member broker/dealers. The purpose of Rule 2711 is to ensure that research reports provided to customers are objective and reliable. This is accomplished by requiring disclosure of conflicts of interest and by prohibiting certain conduct to minimize biased research. Rule 2711 also prohibits investment departments from influencing the work of securities analysts. Rule 2711 governs how securities analysts are compensated for their work. The investment banking department cannot control or influence a research analyst's compensation payment. Research analysts are prohibited from soliciting investment banking and underwriting business. The goal of Rule 2711 is ensure that research reports contain an honest view of the research analyst's recommendations and options.

# Registration of Research Analysts

## Financial Industry Regulatory Authority (FINRA)

FINRA was established in July 2007. FINRA is the consolidation of the National Association of Securities Dealers (NASD) and the regulatory functions of the New York Stock Exchange (NYSE). FINRA is a non-governmental agency that regulates securities firms in the United States. The FINRA is responsible for regulating the securities industry and ensuring that securities firms comply with applicable federal securities laws and SEC rules. The goal is to protect investors and to maintain the integrity of the securities markets. The FINRA performs many functions: Registering employees of member firms, providing education to members and the public, examining member firms, enforcing federal securities laws, reporting securities trades and providing dispute resolution services for investors and member firms. The FINRA also performs market regulation for NASDAQ, the American Stock Exchange, and the International Securities Exchange.

### *Application Process*

Before an individual may apply for the Series 86 and 87 exams, the FINRA member firm that employs the individual must file a Form U4, Uniform Application for Securities Industry Registration or Transfer, with the Central Registration Depository. An individual's registration continues as long as the individual is associated with the member firm that filed the Form U4. Once the Form U4 is filed, the individual must take and pass the exams before the registration is complete. If the individual fails the exams, they must wait 30 days before they can retake the exam. If the same exam is failed three times in a row, the individual must wait 180 days before the exam can be retaken. The results of the exam are reported to the member firm and may include an analysis of the individual's performance.

### *Registration Requirements*

Any individual who is employed by a FINRA member firm and performs the duties of a research analyst is required to register with the FINRA. Before registration as a Research Analyst can become effective, the individual must pass the Securities Industrial Essentials (SIE) exam and the qualification examinations for Research Analysts (Series 86 and 87). Research analysts are those individuals that are primarily responsible for the preparation of research reports or those individuals whose names appear on research reports. The registration requirement only applies to the preparation of research reports for equity securities. Those individuals that act in a support role to a research analyst are exempt from the registration requirement. Support functions may include data preparation and data formatting.

A supervisory analyst is any FINRA member or employee of a member that is responsible for the preparation or approval of research reports. The duties of the supervisory analyst include the review of research reports and ensuring that the research reports comply with the applicable securities rules and regulations. The supervisory analyst may also prepare research reports. In order to be registered as a supervisory analyst, the individual must have the appropriate experience and must pass the Exchange Supervisory Analyst Examination (Series 16). The registration requirement for supervisory analysts only applies to employees of those member firms that conduct business on the New York Stock Exchange (NYSE). If the supervisory analyst also prepares research reports, the individual must pass both the Series 86 and Series 87 exams for qualification as a research analyst.

### Form U4

The information that is required to be disclosed on the Form U4 includes:

- The name and current address of the individual applicant
- Other names which the applicant uses
- The name and current address of the member firm for which the applicant works
- If the applicant is transferring from one member firm to another, the name and current address of the former member firm
- The applicant's residence history for the previous 5 years
- The applicant's employment history for the previous 10 years
- If the applicant is employed by or an owner of any other businesses
- A list of any arrests, convictions, and charges that involve investments, fraud, bribery, and forgery

In addition, if any of the above information changes during the applicant's registration with the FINRA, this information must be disclosed and the Form U4 amended.

### Confidentiality of Examinations

All of the qualification exams (both current and past series) administered by the FINRA are to be kept confidential. Any individual that takes a FINRA qualification exam is prohibited from divulging any information contained in the exam to any other individuals. Any act that compromises the effectiveness of the exam or that reveals exam questions and answers is prohibited. This includes the removal of exam material from the examination center, reproduction of exam material and the passing or receipt of exam information. In addition, an individual is prohibited from receiving any assistance while taking an exam. If a violation occurs, the FINRA will take disciplinary action against individuals that divulge exam materials, individuals that use exam material in the course of taking an exam and their supervisors.

### Continuing Education Requirements

FINRA requires continuing education for all registered individuals. There are two elements to the continuing education requirement, a regulatory element and a firm element:

- The Regulatory Element is a computer-based exam that tests the registered individual on compliance rules, securities regulations and ethical sales practices. FINRA Rule 1240 requires registered persons to complete the Regulatory Element annually by Dec. 31 for each registration that they hold.
- The Firm Element requires that member firms provide formal training programs. The purpose of these training programs is to keep its registered employees current with job and product related subjects. Topics that the member firms should include in the Firm Element of their continuing education program are provided by the Securities Industry Regulatory Council's annual Firm Element Advisory.

A registered individual who does not complete the Regulatory Element within the allotted timeframe will have their status changed to inactive. This inactive status will last until the Regulatory Element has been completed. A registered individual with an inactive status is prohibited from conducting any duties or activities that require registration. If the inactive status lasts for two years, the individual's registered status will be terminated. A terminated registration can only be reactivated by reapplying for registration and by meeting the qualification requirements. This means that to reapply for registration as a research analyst, the individual will need to take and pass the Series 7, Series 86, and Series 87 exams.

### *Situations That Require That the FINRA Be Notified in Writing*

The FINRA requires that member firms notify the FINRA in writing if the firm or registered individuals committed any of the following violations:

- When a securities law has been violated
- When there is a customer complaint that alleges theft, misappropriation of funds or forgery
- When a regulatory authority takes legal action based on a violation of the Securities Acts
- When the firm or an individual is denied registration, expelled, suspended or disciplined by a self-regulatory organization
- When a registered individual is indicted or convicted of a criminal offense (traffic violations and DUIs are exempt)
- When there is an association with an investment or insurance firm which was expelled or suspended from FINRA membership or that was convicted of a felony
- When the firm or individual is a defendant in a securities or commodities related civil litigation or arbitration
- When the registered individual has been disciplined by the firm and which leads to suspension, termination, or a fine

### *Form U5*

If a registered individual voluntarily discontinues employment with a member firm or if the registered individual is terminated, a Form U5 must be filed within 30 days of the termination. Even though the individual is no longer registered, the individual is subject to the jurisdiction of the securities rules and regulations for two years after the date the registration was terminated.

The Form U5 requires the following information:

- Personal information such as name, current address, Central Registration Depository number, and social security number
- Member firm information such as employment address and Central Registration Depository number
- The reason for the termination and the date of the termination
- A disclosure of whether or not the individual was subject to a securities investigation, convicted or charged with any felony or securities violation or was a party in any securities sales practice violation while the individual was registered

## Restrictions Placed on Personal Trading

Research analysts are prohibited from purchasing or selling the securities of a subject company when the following conditions are met:

- The issuer is in the same type of business as companies that the research analyst follows.
- For 30 calendar days before and 5 calendar days after the publication of a research report regarding the issuer or a change in rating or price of the issuer's securities.
- When the purchase or sale would be inconsistent with the research analyst's recommendation published in the recent research report.
- An exception may be made based on a change in the personal finances of the beneficial owner of the research analyst account.

- These restrictions do not apply to the purchase and sale of securities of registered diversified investment companies or investment funds in which the research analyst does not have control.
- Legal or compliance personnel must pre-approve transactions of equity securities of subject companies for persons who oversee research analysts.

## Disclosure Requirements for Financial Interests and Conflicts of Interest

A member broker/dealer must disclose in research reports and a research analyst must disclose in public appearances:

- If the research analyst or a household member has a financial interest in the securities of the subject company. The type of interest must also be disclosed.
- If the member or affiliates own 1% or more of the common equity securities of the subject company.
- Any conflict of interest known on the publication date of the research report.
- If the research analyst received compensation from the subject company in the past 12 months.
- If the member or affiliates managed a public offering for or received compensation for investment banking services from the subject company in the past 12 months.
- If the member or affiliates received compensation for products or services, other than investment banking services, from the subject company in the past 12 months.
- If the research analyst or a household member serves as an officer, director or board member of the subject company.

# Accounting Knowledge and Skills

## Asset Turnover

Asset turnover equals: $\frac{Sales\ (or\ Revenues)}{Total\ Assets}$

It is a way of valuing the amount of sales (or revenues) that are generated off of each dollar of assets. It allows an investor to determine how efficient a company is with their assets. In general, the higher the ratio, the more efficient the company is with their assets.

## Current Ratio

The current ratio equals: $\frac{Current\ assets}{Current\ liabilities}$

The result of this equation indicates to what degree the company can pay its short term debts with its cash on hand. This ratio is also known as working capital.

## Debt to Capital Ratio

The debt to capital ratio equals: $\frac{Debt}{Shareholders'Equity + Debt}$

This is a way to look at the company's overall leverage. In other words, what ratio of a company's overall operations is financed through debt.

## Debt to Equity Ratio

Debt to equity ratio equals: $\frac{Total\ Liabilities}{Shareholders'Equity}$

This is a way to look at how much a company is using debt to finance its operations as compared to equity.

## Dividend Payout Ratio

Dividend payout ratio equals: $\frac{Yearly\ Dividend\ per\ share}{Earnings\ per\ share}$

This is a way to determine what percentage of earnings is paid out to shareholders in the form of dividends.

## Earnings Per Share (EPS)

Earnings per share equals: $\frac{Net\ Income - Dividends\ on\ Preferred\ Stock}{Average\ Outstanding\ Shares}$

This allows an investor to see what amount of profit is allocated to each share of outstanding stock. This is often a tool to see the impact of potential dilution from a stock split.

## EBIT vs. EBITDA vs. EBITDAR

Earnings before interest and taxes (EBIT) is a way of measuring profitability from operations. As the name would suggest, the calculation starts out with earnings before interest and taxes are taken into consideration. Earnings before interest, taxes, depreciation, and amortization (EBITDA) on the other hand, is a way of measuring cash flow. As the name would suggest, this is calculated by looking at earnings before interest, taxes, depreciation, and amortization. It is often used to compare profitability between companies that may choose to finance their organizations through different means or choose a different accounting method. Earnings before interest, taxes, depreciation, amortization, and restructuring or rent costs (EBITDAR) is a method of measuring earnings is often used by organizations that have large rent costs, such as a restaurant; or those which have recently undergone restructuring, which is considered a one-time expense.

### Equity Turnover

Equity turnover is a measurement of how well a company is able to create sales given its equity investment (common stock and preferred stock included).

The formula is: $\frac{Net\ Sales}{Average\ Total\ Equity}$

### Gross Profit Margin

Gross profit margin is a measurement of a company's financial health. It looks to see how much money a company has left from revenues after taking cost of goods sold into consideration.

The formula is: $\frac{Revenue - Cost\ of\ Goods\ Sold}{Revenue}$

### Interest Coverage Ratio

Interest coverage is a ratio that determines the extent to which an organization can pay the interest owed on outstanding debt.

The formula is: $\frac{Earnings\ Before\ Interest\ and\ Taxes}{Interest\ Expense}$

### Net Profit Margin

Net profit margin looks to determine what portion of a company's revenues turns into profits. It is a measure of how well a company can turn its revenue stream into bottom line profits.

The formula is: $\frac{Revenue - COGS - Operating\ Expenses - Interest - Taxes}{Revenue}$

### Pre-Tax Margin

Pre-tax margin looks to determine what portion of a company's pre-tax revenues turns into profits.

The formula is: $\frac{Revenue - COGS - Operating\ Expenses - Interest}{Revenue}$

### Quick Ratio

The quick ratio is: $\frac{Cash\ and\ equivalents + Short\text{-}term\ Investments + Accounts\ Receivable}{Current\ Liabilities}$

This ratio is more conservative than the current ratio because it does not include assets that are more difficult to turn into cash. The quick ratio is also known as the acid test ratio.

### Return on Assets

Return on assets (ROA) measures how profitable a company is in relation to the company's assets. In other words, it looks at how well the company uses assets to create earnings.

The formula is: $\frac{Net\ Income}{Total\ Assets}$

### Return on Equity

Return on equity (ROE) looks at how well a company profits with the money that has been invested by means of shareholders.

The formula is: $\frac{Net\ Income}{Shareholders'Equity}$

### Return on Capital

Return on capital is a measurement of what benefit an investor receives given the cost of the underlying investment.

The formula is: $\frac{Gain\ from\ Investment - Cost\ of\ Investment}{Cost\ of\ Investment}$

### Inventory Valuation

The inventory valuation system is used to determine a company's cost of goods sold. It also allows for a company to include on their financial statements what the cost of the inventory on hand is. The three most common types of inventory valuation systems are last in, first out (LIFO); first in, first out (FIFO); and weighted average cost. LIFO presumes that the assets made or purchased last are the first ones sold or used. FIFO presumes that the assets made or purchased first are the first ones sold or used. With weighted average, the cost is based on an average of all inventory made or purchased. A company chooses which system they want to use at the time of formation.

### Pro Forma and GAAP Reporting

Pro forma reporting is where, for each line item reported on the last financial statement, there is a corresponding line item for the current time period. There are a number of differences between pro forma and GAAP reporting. However, there are four differences in particular that an analyst needs to be on the lookout for:

1. Non-cash items: accruals that are accounting entries which do not have a corresponding cash flow in the same accounting period. This is particularly true in the event of cash that will be paid over a number of accounting periods, as GAAP reporting allows these items to be put in the non-cash category so long as they are not due to be paid in a short-term time period.
2. Write-offs: these are items that are considered impairments, meaning that their existence is bringing down the overall worth of a company. Typically, under GAAP reporting, these are reported as a reduction to the asset with a related expense on the income statement in the form of a capital loss.
3. Mergers: while mergers often bring in additional revenue, there are expenses associated with them as well. Typically, expenses related to a merger will be reported on the income statement on the SG&A line.
4. Discontinued operations: there are special charges associated with a company choosing to discontinue operations under a specific business line. GAAP reporting allows these to be reported on a single line item along with the revenue associated with that operation.

### Receivables Turnover

Receivables turnover measures how quickly and efficiently a company is able to collect outstanding debts, which are in essence interest-free loans.

The formula is: $\frac{Net\ credit\ sales}{Average\ accounts\ receivable}$

### Inventory Turnover

Inventory turnover measures how many times an inventory is sold and subsequently replaced over a specific time period.

There are two different formulas that can be used: $\frac{Sales}{Inventory}$ and $\frac{Cost\ of\ goods\ sold}{Average\ inventory}$

### Payables Turnover

Payables turnover measures the pace at which a company pays its debts to suppliers.

The formula is: $\frac{Total\ supplier\ purchases}{Average\ accounts\ payable}$

# How to Overcome Test Anxiety

Just the thought of taking a test is enough to make most people a little nervous. A test is an important event that can have a long-term impact on your future, so it's important to take it seriously and it's natural to feel anxious about performing well. But just because anxiety is normal, that doesn't mean that it's helpful in test taking, or that you should simply accept it as part of your life. Anxiety can have a variety of effects. These effects can be mild, like making you feel slightly nervous, or severe, like blocking your ability to focus or remember even a simple detail.

If you experience test anxiety—whether severe or mild—it's important to know how to beat it. To discover this, first you need to understand what causes test anxiety.

## Causes of Test Anxiety

While we often think of anxiety as an uncontrollable emotional state, it can actually be caused by simple, practical things. One of the most common causes of test anxiety is that a person does not feel adequately prepared for their test. This feeling can be the result of many different issues such as poor study habits or lack of organization, but the most common culprit is time management. Starting to study too late, failing to organize your study time to cover all of the material, or being distracted while you study will mean that you're not well prepared for the test. This may lead to cramming the night before, which will cause you to be physically and mentally exhausted for the test. Poor time management also contributes to feelings of stress, fear, and hopelessness as you realize you are not well prepared but don't know what to do about it.

Other times, test anxiety is not related to your preparation for the test but comes from unresolved fear. This may be a past failure on a test, or poor performance on tests in general. It may come from comparing yourself to others who seem to be performing better or from the stress of living up to expectations. Anxiety may be driven by fears of the future—how failure on this test would affect your educational and career goals. These fears are often completely irrational, but they can still negatively impact your test performance.

## Elements of Test Anxiety

As mentioned earlier, test anxiety is considered to be an emotional state, but it has physical and mental components as well. Sometimes you may not even realize that you are suffering from test anxiety until you notice the physical symptoms. These can include trembling hands, rapid heartbeat, sweating, nausea, and tense muscles. Extreme anxiety may lead to fainting or vomiting. Obviously, any of these symptoms can have a negative impact on testing. It is important to recognize them as soon as they begin to occur so that you can address the problem before it damages your performance.

The mental components of test anxiety include trouble focusing and inability to remember learned information. During a test, your mind is on high alert, which can help you recall information and stay focused for an extended period of time. However, anxiety interferes with your mind's natural processes, causing you to blank out, even on the questions you know well. The strain of testing during anxiety makes it difficult to stay focused, especially on a test that may take several hours. Extreme anxiety can take a huge mental toll, making it difficult not only to recall test information but even to understand the test questions or pull your thoughts together.

## Effects of Test Anxiety

Test anxiety is like a disease—if left untreated, it will get progressively worse. Anxiety leads to poor performance, and this reinforces the feelings of fear and failure, which in turn lead to poor performances on subsequent tests. It can grow from a mild nervousness to a crippling condition. If allowed to progress, test anxiety can have a big impact on your schooling, and consequently on your future.

Test anxiety can spread to other parts of your life. Anxiety on tests can become anxiety in any stressful situation, and blanking on a test can turn into panicking in a job situation. But fortunately, you don't have to let anxiety rule your testing and determine your grades. There are a number of relatively simple steps you can take to move past anxiety and function normally on a test and in the rest of life.

## Physical Steps for Beating Test Anxiety

While test anxiety is a serious problem, the good news is that it can be overcome. It doesn't have to control your ability to think and remember information. While it may take time, you can begin taking steps today to beat anxiety.

Just as your first hint that you may be struggling with anxiety comes from the physical symptoms, the first step to treating it is also physical. Rest is crucial for having a clear, strong mind. If you are tired, it is much easier to give in to anxiety. But if you establish good sleep habits, your body and mind will be ready to perform optimally, without the strain of exhaustion. Additionally, sleeping well helps you to retain information better, so you're more likely to recall the answers when you see the test questions.

Getting good sleep means more than going to bed on time. It's important to allow your brain time to relax. Take study breaks from time to time so it doesn't get overworked, and don't study right before bed. Take time to rest your mind before trying to rest your body, or you may find it difficult to fall asleep.

Along with sleep, other aspects of physical health are important in preparing for a test. Good nutrition is vital for good brain function. Sugary foods and drinks may give a burst of energy but this burst is followed by a crash, both physically and emotionally. Instead, fuel your body with protein and vitamin-rich foods.

Also, drink plenty of water. Dehydration can lead to headaches and exhaustion, especially if your brain is already under stress from the rigors of the test. Particularly if your test is a long one, drink water during the breaks. And if possible, take an energy-boosting snack to eat between sections.

Along with sleep and diet, a third important part of physical health is exercise. Maintaining a steady workout schedule is helpful, but even taking 5-minute study breaks to walk can help get your blood pumping faster and clear your head. Exercise also releases endorphins, which contribute to a positive feeling and can help combat test anxiety.

When you nurture your physical health, you are also contributing to your mental health. If your body is healthy, your mind is much more likely to be healthy as well. So take time to rest, nourish your body with healthy food and water, and get moving as much as possible. Taking these physical steps will make you stronger and more able to take the mental steps necessary to overcome test anxiety.

## Mental Steps for Beating Test Anxiety

Working on the mental side of test anxiety can be more challenging, but as with the physical side, there are clear steps you can take to overcome it. As mentioned earlier, test anxiety often stems from lack of preparation, so the obvious solution is to prepare for the test. Effective studying may be the most important weapon you have for beating test anxiety, but you can and should employ several other mental tools to combat fear.

First, boost your confidence by reminding yourself of past success—tests or projects that you aced. If you're putting as much effort into preparing for this test as you did for those, there's no reason you should expect to fail here. Work hard to prepare; then trust your preparation.

Second, surround yourself with encouraging people. It can be helpful to find a study group, but be sure that the people you're around will encourage a positive attitude. If you spend time with others who are anxious or cynical, this will only contribute to your own anxiety. Look for others who are motivated to study hard from a desire to succeed, not from a fear of failure.

Third, reward yourself. A test is physically and mentally tiring, even without anxiety, and it can be helpful to have something to look forward to. Plan an activity following the test, regardless of the outcome, such as going to a movie or getting ice cream.

When you are taking the test, if you find yourself beginning to feel anxious, remind yourself that you know the material. Visualize successfully completing the test. Then take a few deep, relaxing breaths and return to it. Work through the questions carefully but with confidence, knowing that you are capable of succeeding.

Developing a healthy mental approach to test taking will also aid in other areas of life. Test anxiety affects more than just the actual test—it can be damaging to your mental health and even contribute to depression. It's important to beat test anxiety before it becomes a problem for more than testing.

## Study Strategy

Being prepared for the test is necessary to combat anxiety, but what does being prepared look like? You may study for hours on end and still not feel prepared. What you need is a strategy for test prep. The next few pages outline our recommended steps to help you plan out and conquer the challenge of preparation.

### Step 1: Scope Out the Test

Learn everything you can about the format (multiple choice, essay, etc.) and what will be on the test. Gather any study materials, course outlines, or sample exams that may be available. Not only will this help you to prepare, but knowing what to expect can help to alleviate test anxiety.

### Step 2: Map Out the Material

Look through the textbook or study guide and make note of how many chapters or sections it has. Then divide these over the time you have. For example, if a book has 15 chapters and you have five days to study, you need to cover three chapters each day. Even better, if you have the time, leave an extra day at the end for overall review after you have gone through the material in depth.

If time is limited, you may need to prioritize the material. Look through it and make note of which sections you think you already have a good grasp on, and which need review. While you are studying, skim quickly through the familiar sections and take more time on the challenging parts.

Write out your plan so you don't get lost as you go. Having a written plan also helps you feel more in control of the study, so anxiety is less likely to arise from feeling overwhelmed at the amount to cover.

## Step 3: Gather Your Tools

Decide what study method works best for you. Do you prefer to highlight in the book as you study and then go back over the highlighted portions? Or do you type out notes of the important information? Or is it helpful to make flashcards that you can carry with you? Assemble the pens, index cards, highlighters, post-it notes, and any other materials you may need so you won't be distracted by getting up to find things while you study.

If you're having a hard time retaining the information or organizing your notes, experiment with different methods. For example, try color-coding by subject with colored pens, highlighters, or post-it notes. If you learn better by hearing, try recording yourself reading your notes so you can listen while in the car, working out, or simply sitting at your desk. Ask a friend to quiz you from your flashcards, or try teaching someone the material to solidify it in your mind.

## Step 4: Create Your Environment

It's important to avoid distractions while you study. This includes both the obvious distractions like visitors and the subtle distractions like an uncomfortable chair (or a too-comfortable couch that makes you want to fall asleep). Set up the best study environment possible: good lighting and a comfortable work area. If background music helps you focus, you may want to turn it on, but otherwise keep the room quiet. If you are using a computer to take notes, be sure you don't have any other windows open, especially applications like social media, games, or anything else that could distract you. Silence your phone and turn off notifications. Be sure to keep water close by so you stay hydrated while you study (but avoid unhealthy drinks and snacks).

Also, take into account the best time of day to study. Are you freshest first thing in the morning? Try to set aside some time then to work through the material. Is your mind clearer in the afternoon or evening? Schedule your study session then. Another method is to study at the same time of day that you will take the test, so that your brain gets used to working on the material at that time and will be ready to focus at test time.

## Step 5: Study!

Once you have done all the study preparation, it's time to settle into the actual studying. Sit down, take a few moments to settle your mind so you can focus, and begin to follow your study plan. Don't give in to distractions or let yourself procrastinate. This is your time to prepare so you'll be ready to fearlessly approach the test. Make the most of the time and stay focused.

Of course, you don't want to burn out. If you study too long you may find that you're not retaining the information very well. Take regular study breaks. For example, taking five minutes out of every hour to walk briskly, breathing deeply and swinging your arms, can help your mind stay fresh.

As you get to the end of each chapter or section, it's a good idea to do a quick review. Remind yourself of what you learned and work on any difficult parts. When you feel that you've mastered the material, move on to the next part. At the end of your study session, briefly skim through your notes again.

But while review is helpful, cramming last minute is NOT. If at all possible, work ahead so that you won't need to fit all your study into the last day. Cramming overloads your brain with more information than it can process and retain, and your tired mind may struggle to recall even previously learned information when it is overwhelmed with last-minute study. Also, the urgent nature of cramming and the stress placed on your brain contribute to anxiety. You'll be more likely to go to the test feeling unprepared and having trouble thinking clearly.

So don't cram, and don't stay up late before the test, even just to review your notes at a leisurely pace. Your brain needs rest more than it needs to go over the information again. In fact, plan to finish your studies by noon or early afternoon the day before the test. Give your brain the rest of the day to relax or focus on other things, and get a good night's sleep. Then you will be fresh for the test and better able to recall what you've studied.

### Step 6: Take a Practice Test

Many courses offer sample tests, either online or in the study materials. This is an excellent resource to check whether you have mastered the material, as well as to prepare for the test format and environment.

Check the test format ahead of time: the number of questions, the type (multiple choice, free response, etc.), and the time limit. Then create a plan for working through them. For example, if you have 30 minutes to take a 60-question test, your limit is 30 seconds per question. Spend less time on the questions you know well so that you can take more time on the difficult ones.

If you have time to take several practice tests, take the first one open book, with no time limit. Work through the questions at your own pace and make sure you fully understand them. Gradually work up to taking a test under test conditions: sit at a desk with all study materials put away and set a timer. Pace yourself to make sure you finish the test with time to spare and go back to check your answers if you have time.

After each test, check your answers. On the questions you missed, be sure you understand why you missed them. Did you misread the question (tests can use tricky wording)? Did you forget the information? Or was it something you hadn't learned? Go back and study any shaky areas that the practice tests reveal.

Taking these tests not only helps with your grade, but also aids in combating test anxiety. If you're already used to the test conditions, you're less likely to worry about it, and working through tests until you're scoring well gives you a confidence boost. Go through the practice tests until you feel comfortable, and then you can go into the test knowing that you're ready for it.

## Test Tips

On test day, you should be confident, knowing that you've prepared well and are ready to answer the questions. But aside from preparation, there are several test day strategies you can employ to maximize your performance.

First, as stated before, get a good night's sleep the night before the test (and for several nights before that, if possible). Go into the test with a fresh, alert mind rather than staying up late to study.

Try not to change too much about your normal routine on the day of the test. It's important to eat a nutritious breakfast, but if you normally don't eat breakfast at all, consider eating just a protein bar. If you're a coffee drinker, go ahead and have your normal coffee. Just make sure you time it so that the caffeine doesn't wear off right in the middle of your test. Avoid sugary beverages, and drink enough water to stay hydrated but not so much that you need a restroom break 10 minutes into the test. If your test isn't first thing in the morning, consider going for a walk or doing a light workout before the test to get your blood flowing.

Allow yourself enough time to get ready, and leave for the test with plenty of time to spare so you won't have the anxiety of scrambling to arrive in time. Another reason to be early is to select a good seat. It's helpful to sit away from doors and windows, which can be distracting. Find a good seat, get out your supplies, and settle your mind before the test begins.

When the test begins, start by going over the instructions carefully, even if you already know what to expect. Make sure you avoid any careless mistakes by following the directions.

Then begin working through the questions, pacing yourself as you've practiced. If you're not sure on an answer, don't spend too much time on it, and don't let it shake your confidence. Either skip it and come back later, or eliminate as many wrong answers as possible and guess among the remaining ones. Don't dwell on these questions as you continue—put them out of your mind and focus on what lies ahead.

Be sure to read all of the answer choices, even if you're sure the first one is the right answer. Sometimes you'll find a better one if you keep reading. But don't second-guess yourself if you do immediately know the answer. Your gut instinct is usually right. Don't let test anxiety rob you of the information you know.

If you have time at the end of the test (and if the test format allows), go back and review your answers. Be cautious about changing any, since your first instinct tends to be correct, but make sure you didn't misread any of the questions or accidentally mark the wrong answer choice. Look over any you skipped and make an educated guess.

At the end, leave the test feeling confident. You've done your best, so don't waste time worrying about your performance or wishing you could change anything. Instead, celebrate the successful completion of this test. And finally, use this test to learn how to deal with anxiety even better next time.

**Review Video: Test Anxiety**
Visit mometrix.com/academy and enter code: 100340

## Important Qualification

Not all anxiety is created equal. If your test anxiety is causing major issues in your life beyond the classroom or testing center, or if you are experiencing troubling physical symptoms related to your anxiety, it may be a sign of a serious physiological or psychological condition. If this sounds like your situation, we strongly encourage you to seek professional help.

## Online Resources

Due to our efforts to try to keep this book to a manageable length, we've created a link that will give you access to all of your online resources:

**mometrix.com/resources719/series8687**

# It's Your Moment, Let's Celebrate It!

Share your story @mometrixtestpreparation